Rapid Graphs with Tabl

Create Intuitive, Actionable Insights
in Just 15 Days

Stephen McDaniel
Principal Analyst, **Freakalytics**™, **LLC**
Faculty, **American Marketing Association**

Eileen McDaniel, Ph.D.
Managing Partner, **Freakalytics**™, **LLC**

Technical Reviewer: **Marc Rueter**
Senior Director of Technology, Consulting and Strategy
Tableau Software™

Cover Design: **Cristy Miller**
Senior Visual Designer
Tableau Software™

*Cover Graphs by Stephen McDaniel with original version feedback by
Ellie Fields and Chris Stolte of* **Tableau Software**™

Please visit us at Freakalytics.com

We have posted many examples of exciting analyses, data visualizations and dashboards that are possible with Tableau Software.

We also offer dynamic, live training in the techniques and tools needed to discover the value long hidden in your data. The ultimate goal of our training is to empower you to make informed decisions and achieve success in your daily work.

Please check our training page for our worldwide public training schedule. We also offer on-site training based on our public courses, which we can tailor to your team's areas of interest and level of experience.

If we can be of help, please contact either Eileen or Stephen at Info@Freakalytics.com or at (206) 588-1678 in the United States.

Acknowledgements

We want to thank the many wonderful people at Tableau that have supported this book and our training- it takes a great company to make such a great product! We'd also like to thank our students- we've enjoyed helping you overcome your data challenges and we still learn something new in every class!

Rapid Graphs with Tableau Software™ 6: Create Intuitive, Actionable Insights in Just 15 Days
Copyright 2009-2011 by Freakalytics, LLC, Seattle, WA

Book edition: 6.0
All examples in this book are from version 6 of Tableau Software.

Printed by CreateSpace, Seattle, WA - an Amazon.com company
Distributed by Freakalytics, LLC

This book is published on-demand, edition numbers may change frequently as the book is updated. Major edition releases will change the digits to the left of the decimal point; minor edition releases will change the digits to the right of the decimal point. For example, changing the book edition from 5.1 to 6.1 is a major release addressing major changes in Tableau Software. Changing the book edition from 5.1 to 5.2 is a minor release of the book, addressing author chosen updates, but likely no significant changes in the Tableau Software release.

Published by:
> **Freakalytics, LLC**
> 3518 Fremont Ave N # 406
> Seattle, WA 98103
> http://www.Freakalytics.com

Table of Contents

Chapter 1 _____ *1*

Tableau Software – how it can change your world _____ *1*

    Power _____ 2

    Speed _____ 5

    Flexibility _____ 7

    Simplicity _____ 9

    Beauty _____ 10

Chapter 2 _____ *11*

Build the core: Tableau basics _____ *11*

    Download, install and open Tableau _____ 12

    Connect to sample data and review the Tableau interface _____ 14

    Show Me! Tableau in action _____ 18

    Categorically clear views _____ 24

Chapter 3 _____ *31*

Go with the flow: more Tableau basics _____ *31*

    Save time with the Tableau toolbar _____ 32

    When tables trump graphs _____ 34

    Insightful maps _____ 38

    View shifting- the underrated histogram and flexible bins _____ 43

    Exporting results to share your insights _____ 49

Chapter 4 _____ 51

Essential view types in Tableau _____ 51

Text Tables- an eye for detail _____ 53

  1. Text Table _____ 53

  2. Highlight Table _____ 54

Heat Maps- how intense is it? _____ 55

Bar Charts- six flavors to meet your needs _____ 56

  1. Aligned Bar _____ 56

  2. Stacked Bar _____ 58

  3. Side-by-Side Bar _____ 59

  4. Bar with Measure on Color _____ 60

  5. Histogram _____ 61

  6. Bullet Graph _____ 62

Chapter 5 _____ 63

Advanced view types in Tableau _____ 63

Line Charts- describe what happened recently _____ 65

  1. Line (Discrete) _____ 65

  2. Line (Continuous) _____ 66

Scatter Plots- relationships matter _____ 67

  1. Circle _____ 67

  2. Scatter (Single) _____ 68

  3. Scatter (Matrix) _____ 69

  4. Dual Axis _____ 71

Gantt Chart- understand the details over time _____ 73

Pie Charts- by popular demand _____ 74

Geographic Maps- what happened where? _____ 76

Combination charts: overlaying multiple charts _____ 77

Chapter 6 _____ 81

Taking over with Tableau - View structure, Marks Card, Summaries, Formatting and Titles _____ 81

Customizing Views from Columns, Rows, Pages and Filters Shelves _____ 82
1. Columns _____ 82
2. Rows _____ 83
3. Pages _____ 83
4. Filters _____ 85
Enhance visual appeal with the Marks card _____ 87
1. Label _____ 87
2. Text _____ 88
3. Color _____ 89
4. Size _____ 91
5. Shape _____ 92
6. Level of Detail _____ 94
The Summary Card- rapid data insights _____ 96
Headers and Axes _____ 97
Titles, Captions, Field Labels and Legends _____ 99
Formatting values in your Views _____ 101

Chapter 7 _____ 103

Organizing the data in your Views- Sorting, Filtering, Aggregations, Percentages, Spotlighting, Totals/Subtotals, and Motion Charts _____ 103

Simple and advanced sorting of views _____ 104
Simple and advanced filtering of views _____ 107
Aggregations for measures- specify the right summaries _____ 109
Percentages provide balance to compare ratios _____ 111
Spotlighting your View to call out important values _____ 112
Totals and Subtotals to sum up parts of your view _____ 114
Motion Charts with Advanced Page Filter Feature _____ 116
    Connect to Data Source, step-by-step _____ *116*

Chapter 8 _____ 123

Essential Calculations and Models- Quick Calculations, Custom Table Calculations, Reference Lines and Trend Lines _____ 123

Quick Table Calculations _____ 124
Custom Table Calculations using data in your views _____ 125
Reference Lines, Bands and Distributions _____ 133
Model your data with Trend Lines _____ 136

Chapter 9   143

Managing data is critical for great results- Data items and data management in Tableau   143

Data items: names, types, roles, properties, attributes and hierarchies   144

View Data- understand the detail behind the view   158

Dividing numeric data items into intervals using bins   159

Grouping dimensions into categories   161

The power of sets to combine and filter your view   164

Chapter 10   167

Advanced data management in Tableau-   167

Calculated Fields, Functions, and Parameters   167

Calculated Field Operators   170

Numeric Functions (Singular)   171

Character Functions (Modify Items)   172

Character Functions (Locate Values in String)   173

Date Functions   174

Type Conversion Functions   176

Logical Functions (If, Then, Else)   177

Aggregate Functions   178

Table Calculation Functions   179

Parameters add additional control for your analysis   180

Chapter 11   183

Advanced data management in Tableau: 183

Managing data connections   183

Queries to retrieve the data you need   184

Data blending to use data from multiple sources in one view   188

Extracts to accelerate your data exploration in Tableau   193

Chapter 12   197

Sharing your insights from Tableau _____ 197

Exporting Images to other applications _____ 198

Exporting Data to other applications and even back to Tableau _____ 200

Print to PDF- export your views to Adobe Acrobat format _____ 204

Packaged Workbooks- take Tableau on the road! _____ 205

Tableau Reader- share packaged workbooks with your colleagues _____ 206

Tableau Server- powerful insights for everyone! _____ 207

Tableau Desktop and Tableau Server _____ 208

Tableau Public –freely share your visual insights with the world! _____ 210

Appendix - Timesaving Tips _____ 212

Stephen's list of valuable keyboard shortcuts _____ 212

Standard Toolbar navigation shortcuts _____ 213

Index _____ 215

Page intentionally left blank for proper book pagination

Chapter 1

Tableau Software – how it can change your world

Power, speed, flexibility, simplicity and beauty

In today's world, we are all trying to make sense of the mountains of data that we encounter every day in our jobs, whether we work in business, IT, government, education, research, or for a non-profit organization. We would like to find a way to quickly and easily get answers from our data, so that we can increase our productivity and make informed decisions about what actions to take. The mission of Tableau is to create easy-to-use software that helps people find these answers and communicate them effectively, whether you are new to analysis or have been analyzing data for years.

Would you like to be able to…

- Quickly build tables and graphs to answer simple questions about your data?

- Answer complex questions about your data with little or no programming?

- Change your tables and graphs on the spot to look how you want, just by clicking on them?

- Give attractive and interactive presentations that not only inform your colleagues, but keep them interested and engaged in what you have to say?

- Do this all with user-friendly software that makes sense to you, and guides you in your analysis or hands you total control, depending on what you need?

Tableau can empower you to do all these things, so you can spend your time looking at your data, instead of trying to figure out your software. Even if you are new to data analysis, you can learn the basics, and possibly some advanced features, in just 15 days if you follow the exercises in this book.

If it seems like we are passionate about what Tableau can help you accomplish- we are! We were motivated to write this book because, at one point, we were just like you- frustrated by the limitations of our data analysis tools and astonished by what we could do so quickly, and so clearly, in Tableau!

We can summarize the strengths of Tableau Software in five words: power, speed, flexibility, simplicity and beauty. Take a look for yourself at the following examples to see what is possible with Tableau!

Power

Whether you are exploring your data for new insights, answering specific questions or even deciding what questions to ask, Tableau gives you unprecedented control to investigate, communicate and take action with the valuable information hidden in your data! Tableau has it all - a wide variety of options to graph your data, the ability to adjust your data so that you are using the right data in the right form for the questions at hand, and a user-friendly interface that's designed around how people think about analysis, allowing you to follow your thoughts as you question and explore your data. You can work with every major data source, from Excel workbooks to the largest databases. You can even extract data from larger sources into a local "extract" file that will make your data exploration more efficient and allow offline analysis when you are away from the office.

Profit and *planned profit by product*
Red is below plan, green is above
Percentage is actual versus plan
Black line in 2010 shows prior year profit amount

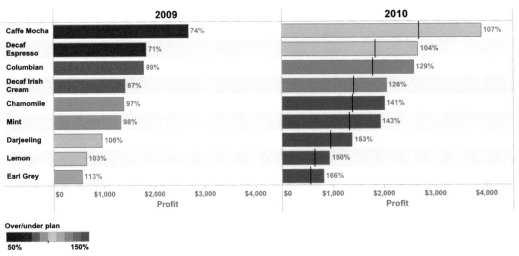

Displaying *profit* versus *sales* by *region* and *customer segment*
Average profit ratio = size of bubble;
Minimum and maximum percents labeled per region
Colors are *customer segments*

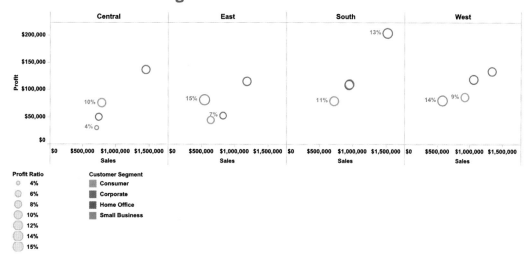

Exploring the relationship of *sales* to *profit* by *region*,
Each point in the graph is a customer order
Colors show the *Customer Segment*
A Trend line is displayed for each *customer segment* per *region*

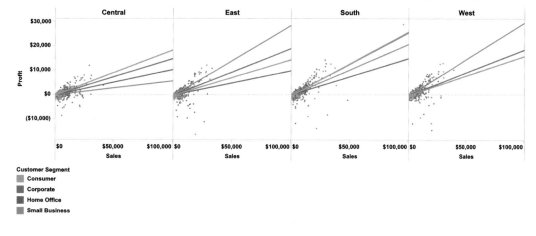

Map of per-capita income growth, 2006 to 2008
Color and size of bubble show growthrate
Labeled states show highest and lowest growth values for country

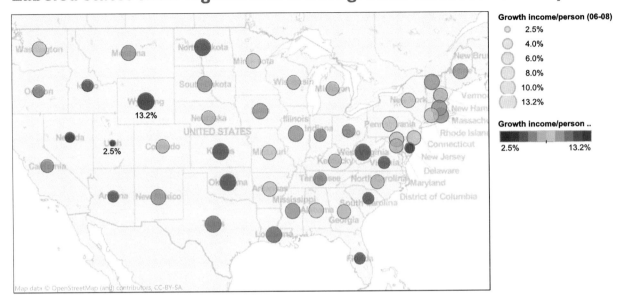

Scatter plot of per-capita income growth by region, 2006 to 2008
Median value for each region shown as reference line
Top and bottom states in each region are labeled

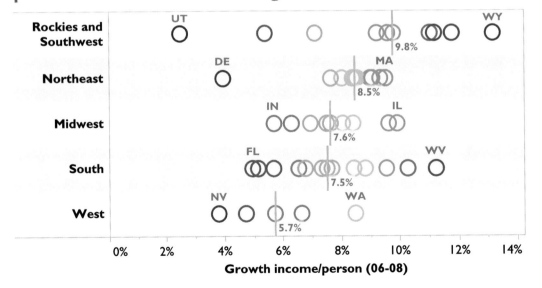

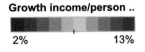

Speed

Faster than you thought possible, you can build presentation quality graphs and tables in Tableau. You can have total control over creating the view or you can ask Tableau to generate the view based on the data that you select. From the view, you can rapidly sort, filter and group the displayed data- with just a few clicks of your mouse. **Each example demonstrates rapid changes made with Tableau in just a few seconds!**

Sales and *profit ratio* by zip code- from bar chart to map with one click!

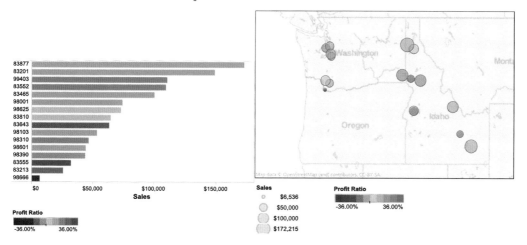

Highlight a data point to quickly examine the values behind it

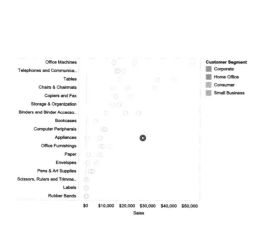

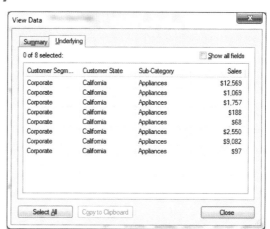

Four views are better than one:
From detailed table to color-highlighted table to side-by-side bar chart to color-encoded bar chart in a minute!

| | | Profit | | | | | | | | Over/under plan | | | | | | | |
| | | 2009 | | | | 2010 | | | | 2009 | | | | 2010 | | | |
		Q1	Q2	Q3	Q4	Q1	Q2	Q3	Q4	Q1	Q2	Q3	Q4	Q1	Q2	Q3	Q4
Central	Coffee	$2,208	$2,473	$2,560	$2,249	$3,330	$3,492	$3,611	$3,341	78%	80%	80%	76%	118%	112%	113%	112%
	Espresso	$2,369	$2,457	$2,481	$2,271	$3,570	$3,477	$3,506	$3,370	72%	73%	71%	55%	108%	104%	101%	82%
	Herbal Tea	$2,414	$2,579	$2,648	$2,450	$3,642	$3,647	$3,738	$3,639	87%	88%	89%	91%	131%	124%	125%	135%
	Tea	$2,118	$2,317	$2,423	$2,245	$3,195	$3,272	$3,424	$3,336	104%	104%	105%	113%	157%	147%	149%	168%
East	Coffee	$2,747	$3,352	$3,740	$2,817	$4,144	$4,732	$5,278	$4,182	95%	96%	95%	99%	144%	136%	134%	147%
	Espresso	$562	$610	$372	$990	$848	$863	$530	$1,469	59%	57%	45%	66%	88%	81%	64%	98%
	Herbal Tea	$591	$922	$522	$592	$889	$1,306	$725	$876	77%	91%	79%	112%	115%	129%	110%	165%
	Tea	$1,480	$1,615	$1,712	$1,537	$2,229	$2,284	$2,419	$2,282	78%	81%	81%	80%	118%	115%	114%	119%
South	Coffee	$1,051	$1,198	$1,312	$1,212	$1,585	$1,692	$1,851	$1,801	61%	62%	64%	59%	92%	87%	90%	87%
	Espresso	$1,465	$1,540	$1,612	$1,498	$2,209	$2,178	$2,279	$2,224	89%	91%	94%	113%	135%	128%	133%	167%
	Herbal Tea	$561	$529	$591	$669	$843	$749	$837	$992	69%	69%	70%	72%	104%	97%	100%	107%
West	Coffee	$1,042	$849	$899	$759	$1,574	$1,201	$1,277	$1,124	44%	40%	40%	35%	67%	56%	57%	52%
	Espresso	$2,325	$2,423	$2,540	$2,439	$3,506	$3,429	$3,589	$3,619	90%	89%	90%	86%	136%	126%	127%	127%
	Herbal Tea	$2,363	$2,739	$2,937	$2,692	$3,566	$3,870	$4,140	$3,996	90%	92%	91%	94%	136%	130%	128%	140%
	Tea	$1,479	$1,585	$1,630	$1,464	$2,228	$2,237	$2,299	$2,176	104%	108%	103%	122%	157%	152%	146%	181%

| | 2009 | | | | 2010 | | | |
	Q1	Q2	Q3	Q4	Q1	Q2	Q3	Q4
Coffee	$7,048	$7,872	$8,511	$7,037	$10,633	$11,117	$12,017	$10,448
Espresso	$6,721	$7,030	$7,005	$7,198	$10,133	$9,947	$9,904	$10,682
Herbal Tea	$5,929	$6,769	$6,698	$6,403	$8,940	$9,572	$9,440	$9,503
Tea	$5,077	$5,517	$5,765	$5,246	$7,652	$7,793	$8,142	$7,794

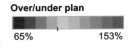

Over/under plan 65% — 153%

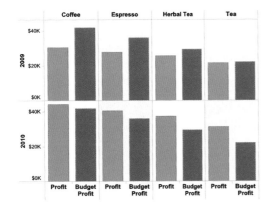

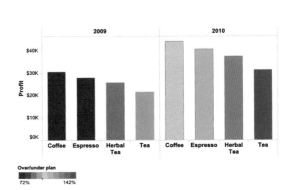

Flexibility

You can easily change any part of your view to look exactly how you want, ranging from data, point shapes and colors to clear data labels to the way your metrics are calculated and compared. The days of thinking of your graphs as "good enough" are a relic of the past with Tableau!

Grouping the data with just a few clicks, from the view!

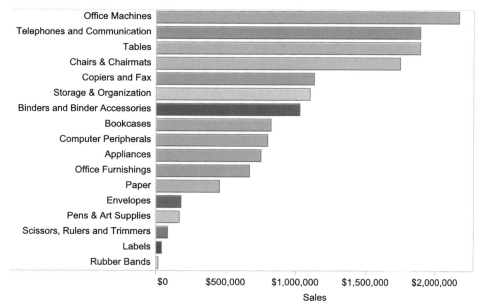

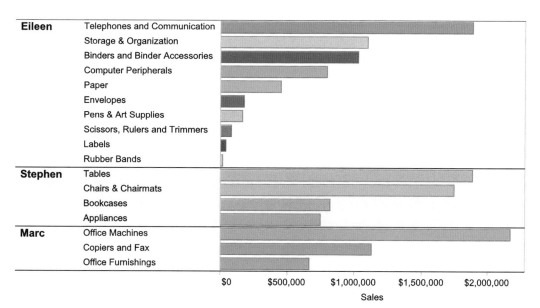

Color code view elements for effective communication

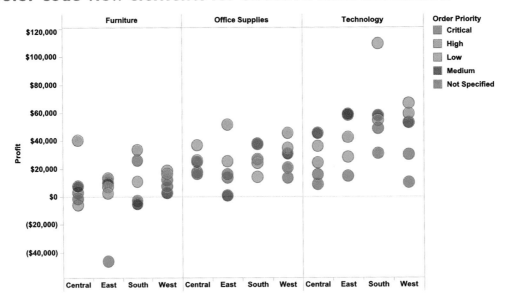

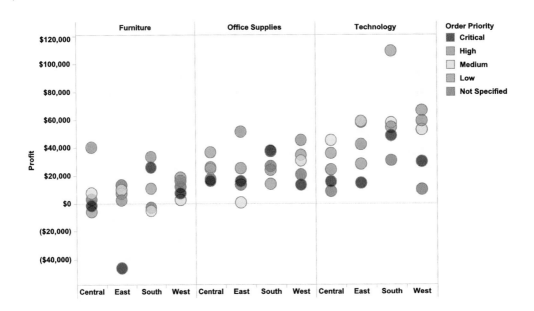

Simplicity

Getting started in Tableau is easy. In the first few weeks, you can learn the basics and begin mastering the techniques of graphical data exploration. Soon you'll discover how to easily create more complex visualizations. You can now investigate those questions that you always wanted to, but thought were impossible!

<u>Areas of simplicity</u>

- Direct interaction with graph- **drag and drop** what you want to see
- **Sort** the data **automatically or manually** directly from the view
- **Simple and complex grouping** of data items categories from the view
- Easily **exclude irrelevant data or keep only** the items of interest from the view
- Quick access to **automated calculations** such as *running total, change over prior year* or *year over year growth* without complex formulas
- Powerful array of advanced **SQL calculations** for almost any need with any data source
- **Table calculations** allow advanced access to manipulate and calculate data items using the data returned from your data source
- Quickly add overall **subtotals**, specific-level subtotals and **grand totals**
- Readily explore the **data summarizing or underlying part of the view** with one click
- Shift from other views to **maps** of the data with one click
- Easily **export** your work to other applications such as **PowerPoint and Word**
- **Free Tableau Reader** allows interactive functionality for those outside your team
- **Publish your work to the web** for wide consumption of results in your company; no installation of any kind is required for web users to have a rich subset of the desktop application functionality

Beauty

Create your own works of art while telling the story of your data in Tableau! Combining powerful insights with beautiful views all in one package will keep your audience engaged and informed during presentations. Tableau also encourages active use of good design principles, making it easy to impress others with effective, clear communications that lead to lively discussions and actionable results. The interactive version of the dashboard below is available at http://www.Freakalytics.com/p/4.

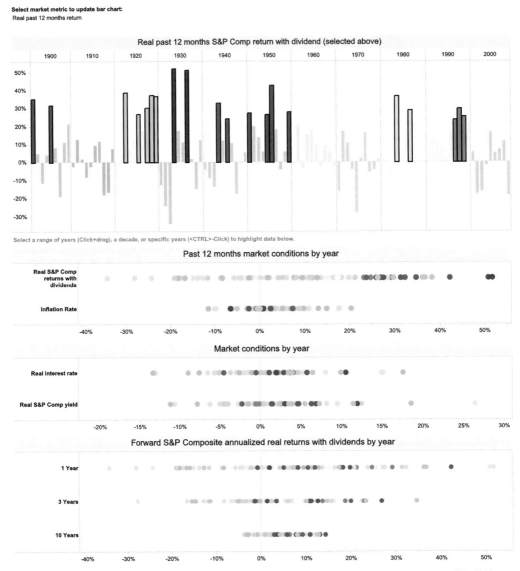

Chapter 2

Build the core: Tableau basics

Chapter Highlights

- Obtaining and setting up Tableau

- Sample data and the Tableau interface

- Your first view of Tableau

- Categorical data never looked so good!

To train for a marathon, you must first walk a mile. The good news is that learning Tableau is much easier than training for a marathon! In this chapter, you will walk through the first "few miles" of Tableau capabilities and even jog through the park a bit.

The first step in learning the basics of Tableau is to become acquainted with the incredibly intuitive application interface. Ironically, one of the greatest challenges as a new user of Tableau is the pleasant surprise at how straightforward it is to use compared to other data visualization applications. Tableau's simplicity and elegance leads you forward with ease while being incredibly flexible and responsive- once you learn the basics.

In the next two chapters, you will cover a broad range of analyses easily available with Tableau. These chapters display a wide array of possibilities while requiring a minimum of detailed application knowledge. At the conclusion of the next chapter, you should be comfortable enough to begin using Tableau in your work.

In this chapter, you will use a sample data source provided by Tableau, the **Sample Coffee Chain** database.

Download, install and open Tableau

If you already have Tableau 6 installed on your PC, you can skip this section and go to the "Connect to sample data and review the Tableau interface" section.

Tableau offers a free software trial if you do not already own a license. The program requires a PC running Microsoft Windows 7, Vista or XP, and you must have administrative rights on your computer to install it. Tableau can also be installed on Windows Server 2000, 2003 or 2008, which is primarily for corporate use on a shared server.

To download a free trial copy of Tableau Professional, **go to** http://www.Freakalytics.com/RapidGraphs.

Before you begin the download, **close all other applications. You should also pause or disable your anti-virus and spyware prevention software.**

Once you click on the "Download Now" link on the Download Desktop page, you will be prompted to save the Tableau Desktop software. When choosing a directory location, save the install file in a directory that is accessible from a user account on your PC with administrative rights. If you are not logged onto your PC as an administrator, log in as a user with administrative rights.

Navigate to the directory where you saved the installation file, and start the installer by double-clicking on it. The Tableau License Agreement dialog appears. You need to **check the box** to accept the license terms and then **click Install.**

The Tableau Setup Welcome dialog

Then, the Activate Tableau dialog appears. **Select "Start trial now", fill out the registration form that appears and click Register.**

The Activate Tableau dialog

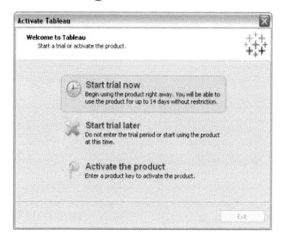

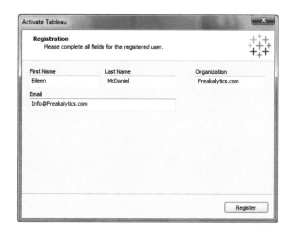

After a few minutes, the installation should be complete and Tableau will automatically start. If you switched accounts to install Tableau, log out as administrator and log back in with your regular user account. Then start Tableau from the Start menu of Windows, **Start → All Programs → Tableau 6**.

You are now ready to begin using Tableau. *Please note that your free trial will last 14 days from the first date you run the application.* If you experience installation problems, consult the Tableau web site at http://www.tableausoftware.com/community/support

Connect to sample data and review the Tableau interface

Open Tableau from the Start menu of Windows, **Start → All Programs → Tableau**. By default, each time you open Tableau you will see the Start page.

The Tableau Start page

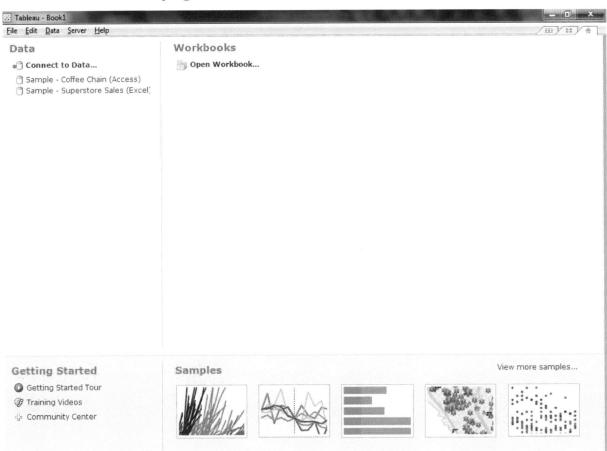

The Start page in Tableau is divided into 4 sections, in addition to the Windows-type menu at the top left. **Data** organizes your data sources, and at this point contains only sample datasets provided by Tableau. The **Workbooks** section usually contains recent workbooks, but currently is empty. **Getting Started** has support links. The **Samples** section has example workbooks provided by Tableau, and if you **click on View more samples** on the right, you can access a large gallery of downloadable workbooks on the web.

In this chapter, you will use a sample data source provided by Tableau, the **Sample Coffee Chain** database. The Sample Coffee Chain is a fictitious national coffee chain. The dataset includes detailed sales, profit, and financial planning data for a 24-month period from January 2009 through December 2010. In the remainder of this chapter, you will answer a number of questions of interest for the management of this company.

Click on the Sample – Coffee Chain (Access) data source from the Start page. The Tableau Workspace opens with the selected data source available for analysis. By default, the workbook is named Book 1.

! *Alternate Route:* All examples in this book use relational data sources, similar to Excel worksheets, Access tables or an Oracle database table. It is important to note that Tableau behaves differently in various parts of the application when using multi-dimensional data sources or "Cubes" (also called Microsoft Analysis Services, Essbase and other vendor names) as your data source. Although the vast majority of functionality is consistent across all databases, Tableau has specific features that are designed to leverage the benefits of each type of database while working within the constraints of each data source. If you are using one of these less common data sources and encounter different dialogs than those shown, **please consult the Tableau Online Help from Help → Help or by clicking F1.**

The Tableau Workspace with key areas highlighted

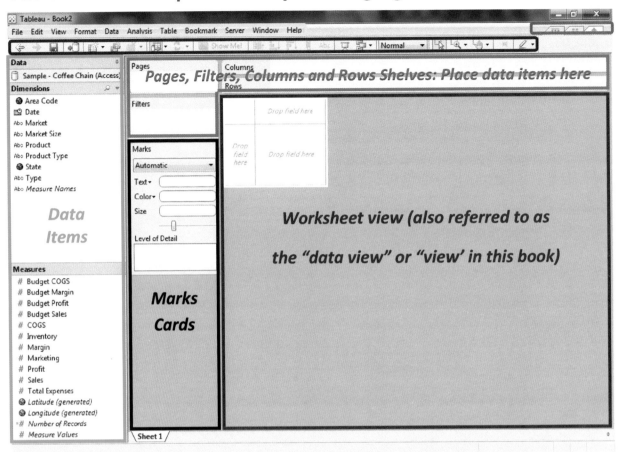

The Tableau Workspace has two standard features common to all Windows applications, the **file menu**, outlined in yellow above, and a **toolbar** below it, outlined in purple. Both behave as they normally do in Windows. The functions found on the various dropdowns of the file menu will be covered as you progress throughout the book, and the toolbar is shown in detail in the next chapter. The **workspace controls**, the three tabs at the top right of the workspace in the pink box, are discussed below.

Specific to Tableau, there are **four key sections** of the interface:

1. Data Items pane (outlined in green): shows the data source in use, offers a search box for data items or fields called Find Field (just click on the magnifying glass icon), and divides the data items available in the data source into **Dimensions** and **Measures**. Dimensions can be thought of as data "organizers" or "categories". Examples include location, date, product, and customer identifiers. Measures are measurements or calculations using your data. Examples include sales amount, profit, inventory on hand, cost of goods, and number of (data) records. In examples throughout the book, dimensions and measures are highlighted with green, bold, and italicized text, e.g., *Dimension* or *Measure*.

2. Marks Card/s (black): in Tableau, data are displayed by **marks**, where every mark, or data point, represents a row or group of rows found in the original data source. These cards allow you to control how the data items are presented in the Worksheet space. For example, for selected marks, you can specify shapes, whether or not to display text or labels, colors, and sizes such as the width of the mark.

3. Pages/Filters/Columns and Rows Shelves (blue): where data items of interest are placed to control the data summarized in the Worksheet view.

4. Worksheet view, data view, or view (red): where the summarized data are displayed in tables or graphs. This is where all of your requests come together for your review and analysis or for presentation to colleagues.

Workspace Controls

At the top right of your screen, underneath the minimize, maximize and exit buttons, there are three tabs- the **workspace controls** (outlined in pink on the workspace screenshot). You can use them to toggle between various screens in Tableau. The first one, with three squares sandwiched in between two lines, brings up the Tableau Workspace. The second one, with four squares, is a "worksheet sorter" that shows thumbnail pictures of the various worksheets you are working on, so you can select the one you want. The third one, the house, brings you back "home" to the Tableau Start Page.

Show Me! Tableau in action

The CFO of the Sample Coffee Chain is interested in a simple two-year view of sales, profit, and profit versus planned profit by month. She would like this information on one page for her monthly team reviews so she can hand it out without wasting too much paper. Additionally, she wants it to be very easy to contrast the current year with the prior year. In this first example, you will create this view.

1. **While holding down the <Ctrl> key on your keyboard, move your mouse to the Data Items pane and click on** *Date* **in the Dimensions section and** *Sales* **in the Measures section**. The <Ctrl> key allows you to select multiple data items at one time. **Click Show Me!** on the toolbar. The Show Me! dialog will appear with the Line (Discrete) graph type automatically selected by Tableau (if you hover over the icons of the different data views the type will appear). **Click OK.**

The Show Me! dialog defaults to the Line (Discrete) graph type

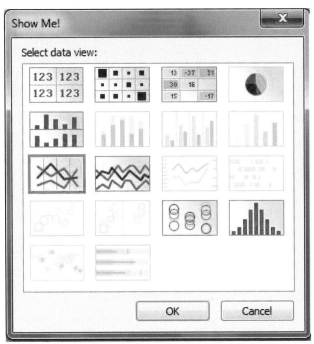

The initial view- *Sales* by *Year*

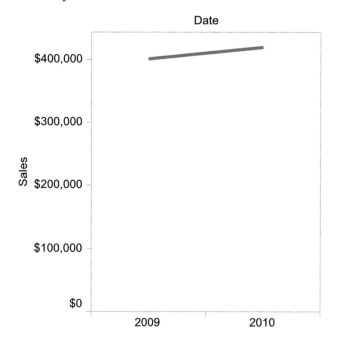

Note that even though *Date* is at the month level in the dataset, the data view automatically started at the year level. Dates in Tableau default to a hierarchical arrangement- Year, Quarter, Month and Day.

In addition, *Sales* became *Sum(Sales)* on the Rows shelf. In this case, the sales values displayed in the view are *sums* of individual sales values. This will make more sense as you learn Tableau, but how the data item is displayed on the shelves lets you know how Tableau *aggregates* the data shown in the view.

2. In data analysis software, to "drill down" means to move from a summarized data item to a more detailed view of the item (if more levels of detail exist). Drill down from an annual view to a quarterly and monthly view of the data. You can drill down on dates by **clicking the + (Plus) sign immediately before the** *Date* **variable in the Columns shelf** (near the center of the Workspace under the toolbar). **Click on the + sign for** *Year*. *Quarter* will appear to the right on the Columns shelf and visually in the Worksheet. **Click on the + sign for** *Quarter*. *Month* also will appear on the shelf and in the Worksheet view.

! *Alternate Route:* To drill down, you can hover over the *Date* data labels directly in the view and click on the + sign that appears to the left of the axis.

Use the plus sign on drillable data items to drill down

The view after drill-down - *Sales* by *Year*, *Quarter*, and *Month*

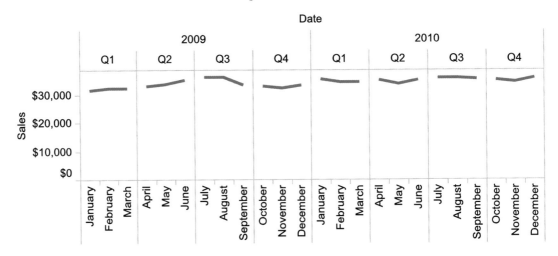

3. Since *Quarter* makes this view busy, remove it. **Click on** *Quarter(Date)* **in the Columns shelf and without releasing the click, drag** *Quarter(Date)* **to any spot on the screen except for the graph, shelves or Marks Card, and then release it** (this is called "drag and drop"). Notice how the view dynamically updates with each action.

! *Alternate Route*: You can hover over the *Quarter(Date)* data labels (Q1, Q2, etc.) directly in the view, and when a triangle (the "drag handle") appears to the left with a four-direction arrow, drag and drop it in Data Items pane.

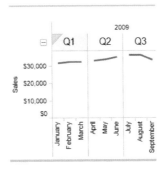

! *Performance Tip*: When you drag and drop, you do not need to drop the item in any specific place – as soon as a little red X appears, when you drop the data item, it will be removed from the view.

4. Since we intend to contrast year over year changes, you can color code the different years by using the *Year* level of the *Date* data item. **Drag and drop** *Year* **from the Columns shelf**, **or the drag handle for** *Year* **in the view, onto the Color shelf on the Marks Card.** Looks good!

The view with *Year* contrasted by color coding

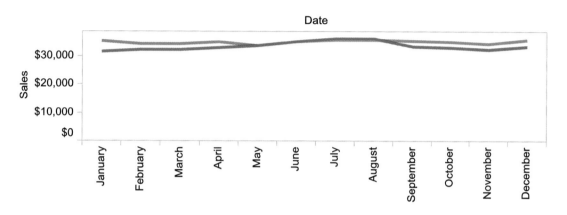

5. **Drag the** *Profit* **data item to the Rows shelf and drop it after the** *Sales* **data item.** This demonstrates how any view can be built using drag and drop in place of the Show Me! Button.

Sales contrasted with *Profit*

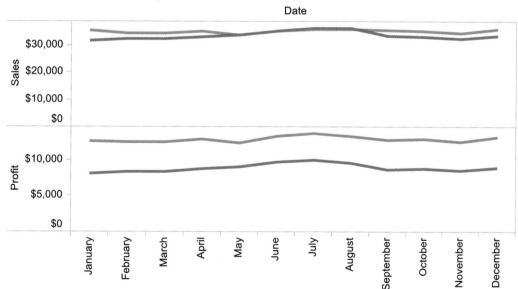

6. Finally, notice there is no data item that compares profit and planned profit. There are *Profit* and *Budget Profit* data items. You can use these two data items to create a calculated data item, *Profit vs. Plan*. **Right-click on** *Profit* **in the Data Items pane and a context menu appears. Select Create Calculated Field from the menu**. The Calculated Field dialog appears.

The Calculated Field dialog with the formula for *Profit vs. Plan*

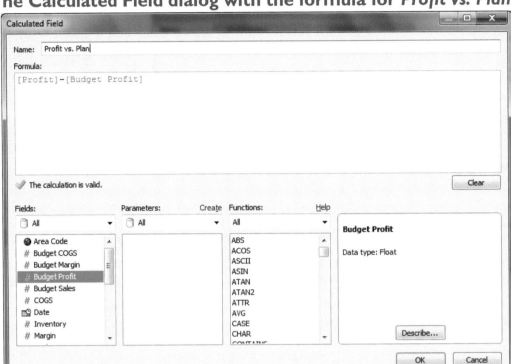

7. In the Formula pane of the Calculated Field, the data item *Profit* is preselected for the formula. After [Profit], **add a – (minus) sign and then double-click on** *Budget Profit* in the Fields section of the dialog. The formula should now read, "[Profit] - [Budget Profit]". Tableau automatically checks the formula for validity- since this formula is valid, a green check appears next to the statement "The calculation is valid." In the **Name section at the top of the dialog, change the name to "Profit vs. Plan"**. **Click OK**. The new calculated field appears in the Measures section of the Data Items pane, with an equals sign, =, to the left of the name, to signify that it is a calculated data item.

8. **Add the calculated data item** *Profit vs. Plan* **to the Rows shelf after the** *Profit* **data item**. The worksheet is now complete! Note the **status bar** at the far bottom left of the workspace, which describes what you have in the current view. There are 72 marks in 3 rows (*Sales*, *Profit*, and *Profit vs. Plan*) by 12 columns (12 months) and *Sum of Profit vs. Plan* across the 24 marks (2 years, one year below and one year above overall) is $783.

The analysis requested by Sample Coffee Chain's CFO

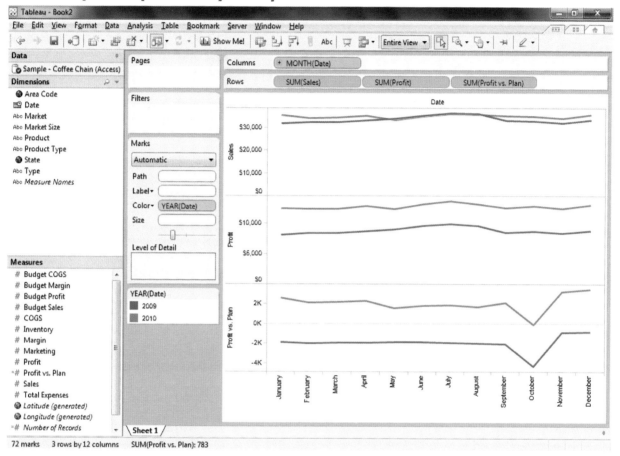

A very informative view:

- The "Sales" graph shows that sales are barely higher in 2010 than in 2009, with the summer being flat year over year.

- However, if you look at the "Profit" graph, 2010 has much higher profit levels than 2009. Apparently, in 2010, the company either controlled expenses better or increased prices or sales volume enough to boost profits 40-50%.

- Finally, the "Profit vs. Plan" graph suggests that the company has some quirks in budget planning because the projected profits were inaccurate. There is usually a difference between actual and planned profits (except in October 2010). The good news is that the company is significantly above planned 2010 profits, a welcome improvement from 2009 where it was always below planned profits. Unfortunately, a spike in profitability was planned for both years, something that should be adjusted or removed in the plan for 2011.

To make it easy for the CFO to use this analysis, you have four options. The CFO could use Tableau (the best choice!) or the free Tableau Reader downloadable from the Tableau website. You could export the view to a PDF by **selecting the File → Print to PDF menu item.** You could also copy the view as an image, by **right-clicking on the Worksheet view and selecting Copy Image.** If you want the view in PowerPoint, the Copy Image feature is the best route. When you select this option, you will be prompted for details about what parts of the view to export and details about legend usage in the copied image.

Categorically clear views

The regional sales managers of Sample Coffee Chain are interested in an analysis of profit by product. They will use these data to discuss growth opportunities for new products and possible pricing changes or product cancellation ideas. Here you will create a simple view to show profitability by product.

1. **Click on the Edit menu and select New Worksheet.** A new worksheet is added to the project, named Sheet 2 by default.

2. **While holding down the <Ctrl> key on your keyboard, move your mouse to the Data Items pane and click on** *Product* **in the Dimensions section and** *Profit* **in the Measures section. Click Show Me!** on the toolbar. The Show Me! dialog will appear with the Aligned Bar graph type automatically selected by Tableau. **Click OK.** A bar chart with profit by product is generated in the Worksheet view.

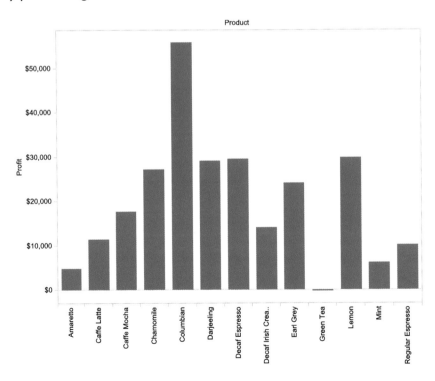

3. To highlight the highest profit products, sort the bars by profit. If you hover with your mouse over the *Product* oval on the Columns Shelf, a down caret appears. **Click on the down caret and select Sort from the drop down context menu.** The Sort dialog opens.

The down caret for accessing the context menu

The context menu available from dimensions placed on the shelf

4. The Sort dialog has the default settings of Sort Order: Ascending for Sort by field Data Source Order. **Change the Sort Order to Descending and the Sort by to Field.** *Profit* **is already selected in the drop down. Click OK**. The bar graph is now sorted in descending profit order by each product.

The Sort dialog for *Product*

! *Alternate Route:* You will learn more about sorting your data in a later chapter, but a quick shortcut to sorting measures that are currently in use is to use the Sort Ascending and Sort Descending buttons on the toolbar, which look like this:

5. Since the regional managers will be interested in the performance of their respective markets, you should add *Market* to the Rows Shelf to the left of the *Profit* data item already in place. **Drag and drop *Market* just to the left of *Profit*.** Tableau indicates where the item will drop by displaying a tiny blue inverted caret behind the *Market* field. Note that the sorting is based on the overall profit across all four regions, not any particular region!

Profit by *Product* and *Market/Region*

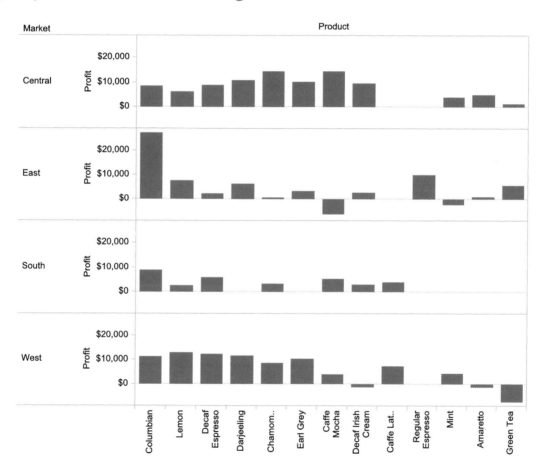

6. To highlight profitability levels, **add** *Profit* **directly from Data Items to the Color shelf of the Marks Card** (do not drag it from the Rows Shelf because your bar chart with be converted to a table). Tableau automatically uses a red-green contrast to show negative profitability as red and positive profitability as green. Tableau also uses the intensity of the two colors to show lower or higher values. The result is that lower and higher values stand in great contrast.

! *Alternate Route*: **Drag** *Profit* **to the center of the view and Tableau will automatically add it to the Color shelf,** because dragging a field to the center will "add it" to the sheet using Show Me! Rules.

Profit by *Product* and *Market/Region* with *Profit* color-encoded

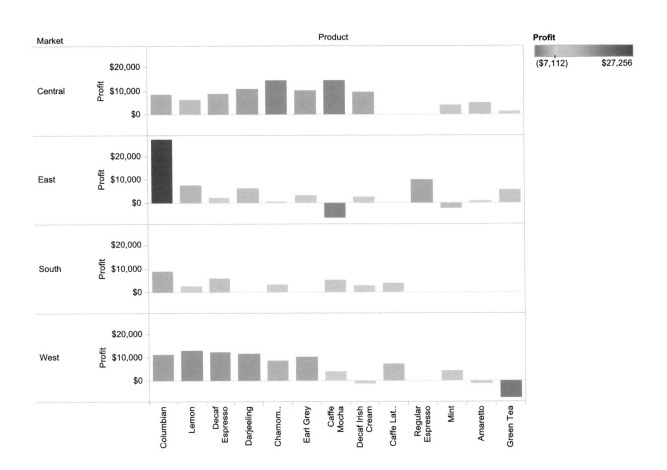

7. Finally, since the regional managers are interested in understanding profitability of various products in their own regions, the distribution shape of each region is informative. However, it is likely even more informative to color encode the value by the profit results versus the planned profit results. Why? This is because pricing may not result in the high profits that are expected for certain products. To enable this view, one simple change is required- **on the Color shelf, replace** *Profit* **by dragging and dropping** *Profit vs. Plan* on top of it.

Profit by *Product* and *Market* with *Profit vs. Plan* color-encoded

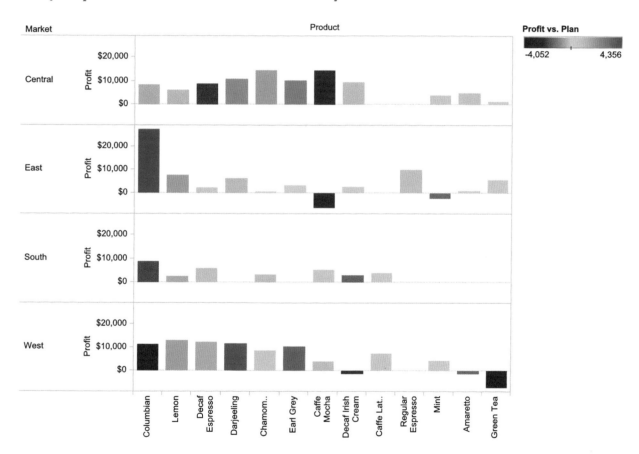

This final view reveals a great amount of information. The overall shape of profitability varies across the four regions with no clear pattern. Additionally, some of the highest profit items in the regions are often the worst performing products relative to plan (for instance, Café Mocha in the Central Region). This information would likely lead to widely varying regional opinions about future product directions. This might inform the team that product line strategy should be managed at the regional level.

Page intentionally left blank for proper book pagination

Chapter 3

Go with the flow: more Tableau basics

Chapter Highlights

- Get mileage out of the Tableau toolbar!

- Table the data for an in-depth view

- Maps and geographical results

- View shifting with histograms and bins

- Sharing the insights created in Tableau

Now that you have performed some analysis with Tableau and are familiar with the feel and general workflow, you are ready to review more of the application. The regional sales managers and product planners have seen your initial results and they are excited and ready to pepper you with more questions.

In this chapter, first you will learn about the many useful shortcuts found on the Tableau toolbar. Then, you will get back to the task at hand, answering colleagues' questions by creating advanced tables, and insightful maps, and transforming histograms into advanced bar charts to get your point across to your audience. The chapter concludes with a brief overview of the many ways that you can deliver your Tableau findings to your team, customers, and external parties.

In this chapter, you will use a sample data source provided by Tableau, the **Sample Coffee Chain** database.

Save time with the Tableau toolbar

Tableau has only one toolbar. You can perform many common actions quickly by clicking the buttons on the toolbar.

The Tableau Toolbar

We have included useful information about the toolbar buttons in the following table.

Button	Name	Action	Shortcut Keys/ Alternative Routes
	Undo and Redo	Undo or redo last action Both can be used repeatedly	**Undo:** <Ctrl> + Z **Redo:** <Ctrl> + Y
	Save	Save workbook	<Ctrl> + S
	Connect to Data	Connect to data sources such as Excel or Access	<Ctrl> + D
	New sheet, Duplicate sheet, Clear sheet	Whole worksheet actions	**New:** <Ctrl> + M **Duplicate:** Main Menu → Edit **Clear:** <Ctrl> + <Alt> + Backspace
	Automatic Update, Run Update	Data source query	**Automatic:** F10 toggles on/off **Run:** F9; use to update when automatic is turned off
	Show Me!	Available view options	<Ctrl> + 1
	Swap	Exchanges rows and columns	<Ctrl> + W

Button	Name	Action	Shortcut Keys/ Alternative Routes
	Sort Ascending, Sort Descending	Manual sort of a particular data item	Right-click on the header of a dimension and sort options will appear
	Group Members	Creates new data item from two or more individual dimensions	Right-click on a dimension and select **Create Group**
Abc	**Show Mark Labels**	Labels data points with names or values	On the **Marks Card** → **Label shelf** dropdown, check the **Show Mark Labels** box
	Presentation Mode	Hides everything except for the view, legends and quick filters	<Ctrl> + H
	View Cards	View Cards dropdown menu, for changing cards and shelves	**Main menu→ View** has some of the options
Normal	**Fit selector**	Dropdown sizes the view- options are Normal, Fit Width, Fit Height, Entire	Manually resize by dragging borders of the view
	Select, Zoom, Pan	Navigation tools for data inspection	**Select:** <Shift> + F6 **Zoom:** <Shift> + F9 **Pan:** <Shift> + F7
	Fix Axes	Toggle button that clears specific axes to a selected range or displays the entire	Right-click on axis and select **Edit Axis** menu
	Highlight	Menu with options for turning highlighting on/off	<Ctrl> + Select marks to highlight directly within the view

! Performance Tip: Be certain to make good use of the table of useful keyboard shortcuts in the appendix. These can save you even more time in your daily analysis work with Tableau.

When tables trump graphs

After the regional sales managers reviewed your analysis of profit by product, the West sales manager called and asked for more details. He said that his area managers could not agree on the weak and strong products and they were interested in whether the differences might be understood by examining product profit by small versus major markets. To examine the details, you will use a "heat map" color-coded data table. Heat map color-coding uses color to represent or highlight the values or intensities of variables so that minimum and maximum values stand out.

1. **On the Start menu, open the Sample-Coffee Chain (Access) data source, or, if you still have it open from the last exercise, click on the Edit menu and select New Worksheet**. A new worksheet is added to the project.

2. **While holding down the <Ctrl> key on your keyboard, move your mouse to Data Items and click on *Date*, *Market Size* and *Product* in the Dimensions area and *Profit* in the Measures area. Click Show Me!** on the toolbar. The Show Me! dialog will appear with the Line (Discrete) graph type automatically selected by Tableau. **Change the data view to Text Table (Crosstab) in the upper left corner and click OK**. A Text Table will appear in the Worksheet view. You can find the rest of the table by **clicking on the scroll bar along the bottom of the table.**

Profit by *Market Size* by *Year*

	Product / Date											
	Amaretto		Caffe Latte		Caffe Mocha		Chamomile		Columbian		Darjeeling	
Market Size	2009	2010	2009	2010	2009	2010	2009	2010	2009	2010	2009	2010
Major Market	$746	$1,203	$2,384	$3,470	$4,005	$5,684	$4,531	$6,732	$17,996	$26,065	$5,437	$7,779
Small Market	$1,237	$1,704	$2,252	$3,269	$3,196	$4,793	$6,562	$9,406	$4,781	$6,962	$6,407	$9,430

3. Since we are examining the West region only, **drag *Market* from the Dimensions area of the Data Items and drop it on the Filters shelf**. The Filter dialog will appear. **Click on "West" and click OK**.

The Filter Dialog

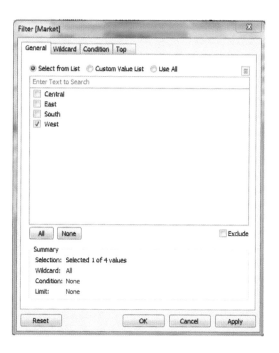

! Performance Tip: If you are working with a large or slow database, filter the data before you add any items to the view (after Step 1 in this section).

4. Since you are particularly interested in the products with negative profit, color encode the profit data by **dragging** *Profit* **from the Measures area of the Data Items to the Color shelf of the Marks Card.**

    a. By default, a measure with negative and positive values will encode the negative values as red and the positive values as green.

    b. The color encoding is coloring only the text of the profit values, not the background of the cells. To amplify the highlighting of the profit values, add some color encoding of the cells, **Click on Show Me! and change the graph type to "Highlight Table" and click OK**.

Profit by *Market Size* and *Year* with Color Highlighting (West Markets only)

							Product / Date						
	Amaretto		Caffe Latte		Caffe Mocha		Chamomile		Columbian		Darjeeling	
Market Size	2009	2010	2009	2010	2009	2010	2009	2010	2009	2010	2009	2010
Major Market	($912)	($1,305)	$1,834	$2,663	$362	$524	$1,328	$1,924	$3,498	$5,068	$1,393	$2,025
Small Market	$402	$591	$1,224	$1,781	$1,294	$1,886	$2,280	$3,322	$1,095	$1,595	$3,407	$4,959

5. Drill down on the *Date* data item by **clicking on the + sign to the left of the word** *Year*. *Quarter(Date)* appears next to the *Year(Date)* data item.

6. To enable easier comparison of year over year changes in profit by quarter, move quarters to the rows side of the Text Table by **dragging the** *Quarter* **data item from the Columns shelf and dropping it on the Rows shelf next to** *Market Size*.

7. To summarize the profit across both market sizes for each year, turn on the column totals. **Click on Table on the main menu and choose "Column Grand Totals".**

8. To emphasize not just profit level, but growth or reduction in profit year over year, change the color-coding to year over year growth rate in profit. **On the Marks Card, click on the down caret that appears when you hover over the Color box labeled "SUM(Profit)".** A context menu appears. **Scroll to Quick Table Calculation** near the bottom of the menu and a submenu appears- **click on Year over Year Growth.**

Context Menu and Submenu for Profit Color Coding

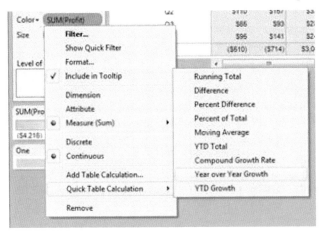

Profit by *Market Size* for **West Markets** by *Year* and *Quarter,*
Color Highlighting by Year over Year Growth

		Product / Date											
		Amaretto		Caffe Latte		Caffe Mocha		Chamomile		Columbian		Darjeeling	
Market Size	Quarter of D..	2009	2010	2009	2010	2009	2010	2009	2010	2009	2010	2009	2010
Major Market	Q1	($70)	($104)	$431	$650	$70	$105	$303	$457	$766	$1,156	$291	$438
	Q2	($273)	($385)	$478	$676	$87	$124	$350	$494	$928	$1,310	$327	$461
	Q3	($351)	($492)	$490	$692	$121	$170	$387	$545	$1,051	$1,484	$379	$538
	Q4	($218)	($324)	$435	$645	$84	$125	$288	$428	$753	$1,118	$396	$588
Small Market	Q1	$132	$200	$354	$534	$268	$404	$587	$887	$281	$425	$852	$1,287
	Q2	$110	$157	$339	$480	$278	$393	$561	$794	$261	$369	$840	$1,189
	Q3	$65	$93	$288	$406	$326	$463	$552	$780	$288	$409	$892	$1,260
	Q4	$95	$141	$243	$361	$422	$626	$580	$861	$265	$392	$823	$1,223
Grand Total		($510)	($714)	$3,058	$4,444	$1,656	$2,410	$3,608	$5,246	$4,593	$6,663	$4,800	$6,984

- Since the light red cells are negative profit growth quarters (year over year), a quick review of this table highlights the fact that unprofitable market sizes in 2009 have become even more unprofitable in 2010, a troubling trend.

- Likewise, market sizes that were profitable in 2009 are even more profitable in 2010, a good trend.

- The table highlights that unprofitable products overall are always profitable in at least one of the two overall market sizes. This is a bit surprising and perhaps indicative of the need for further research and possible modification needed in market-based offering decisions.

! Performance Tip: The Marks card, which you used in this example, is a very powerful tool that you can use to quickly alter the appearance of the items in your view. It is covered in detail in a later chapter.

Insightful maps

After the regional sales managers reviewed your analysis of profit by product, they scheduled a follow-up meeting and asked for a map to distribute to the state managers. The CEO's request: "Maps are all the rage on the web. We want to distribute the state-by-state results on a map that is simple to understand. Show us how well each manager adjusted their profitability plans after an abysmal job planning profitability in 2009!"

To meet this specific request, you will use a "Map" view with color-coded values for profit versus plan.

1. On the keyboard, **select <Ctrl> and M at the same time to add a New Worksheet (abbreviated <Ctrl>-M from now on)**.

2. **While holding down the <Ctrl> key on your keyboard, move your mouse to Data Items and click on** *Date* **and** *State* **in the Dimensions area and** *Profit* **in the Measures area. Click Show Me!** on the toolbar. The Show Me! dialog will appear with the Map graph type automatically selected by Tableau. **Click OK**. A map of *Profit* (shown by the size of the bubbles or "size-encoded") by *State* and *Year* will appear.

! *Performance Tip:* Note that if you are offline, a dialog box will pop up saying that you cannot load the online map. **Click OK and select Data → Background Maps → Offline.**

Profit by State and Year, Profit is Size-Encoded (bubble size)

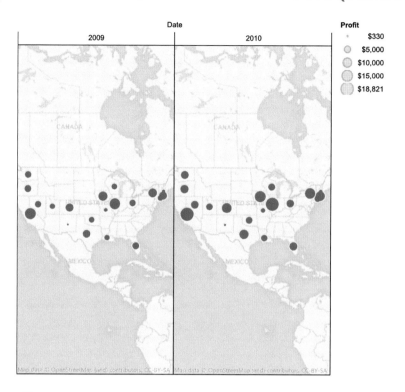

! *Alternate Route:* After Step I in this section, **double-click on** *State*, *Date* **and** *Profit*.

3. The maps would be easier to look at if they were stacked rather than side-by-side. **Drag** *Year(Date)* **from the Columns shelf and drop it on the Rows Shelf to the left of the** *Latitude (Generated)* **data item**. The map view updates with the 2009 map placed above the 2010 map.

4. You should now have the states with the biggest profits already displayed. It will be useful to highlight their performance by comparing them with planned profits. To add *Profit vs. Plan* to the view, **drag and drop** *Profit vs. Plan* **from Data Items to the Color shelf in the Marks Card.**

5. The bubbles for each state are now color-encoded based on the size of the difference in dollars of profit versus planned profit (or how off the plans were!). The sizes of the bubbles did not change (they still represent profit only). Deep red is very bad (the planned profits were way above the actual profits!), red is bad, gray is neutral (expected), light green is good (exceeded plan), and dark green is very good. Note that this not only makes it easy to see the most profitable states quickly, it also makes finding the states with the worst and best performance relative to plan very easy.

Profit by State by Year, Color Encoding of Profit versus Plan

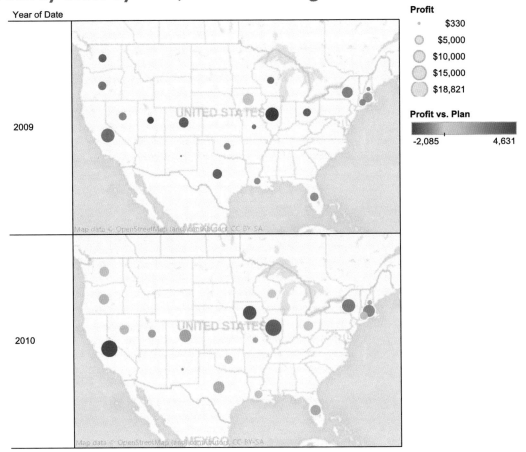

6. Since managers are often very interested in the details of just how far off their plans were from the outcome, you can give them this information in the map as a ratio of profit vs. planned profit. Create a new calculated data item, *Profit as a % of Plan*. **Right-click on** *Profit* **in the Data Items pane**. A context menu appears. **Select Create Calculated Field from the menu**. The Calculated Field dialog appears.

7. In the Formula pane of the Calculated Field, the data item *Profit* is preselected for the formula. **Edit the formula so that it reads:**
   Sum([Profit]) / Sum([Budget Profit])

8. In the **Name section of the dialog, change the name to "Profit as a % of Plan"**. **Click OK**. The new calculated field appears in the Measures part of the Data Items pane.

9. **Add the calculated data item** *Profit as a % of Plan* **to the Label shelf of the Marks Card**.

10. Since you want this metric to be displayed as a percentage, you should format it. **Right-click on** *Profit as a % of Plan* **in the Label shelf of the Marks Card.** A context menu appears. **Select Format from the menu.** The Format pane replaces the Data Items pane on the left side of the Tableau application.

The Format Pane

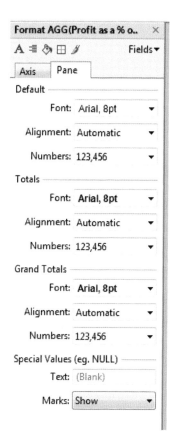

11. Under the Default heading, **click on the dropdown (the down carat) in the Numbers selector.** A dialog appears. **Select Percentage and change the Decimal places setting to "0". To close the Format Pane, click on the "x" in the upper right corner.** The Data Items pane reappears to the left of the final map, which is shown below.

Size encoding *Profit* by *State* and *Year*,
Color Encoding of *Profit versus Plan*, Text Showing *Profit as a % of Plan*

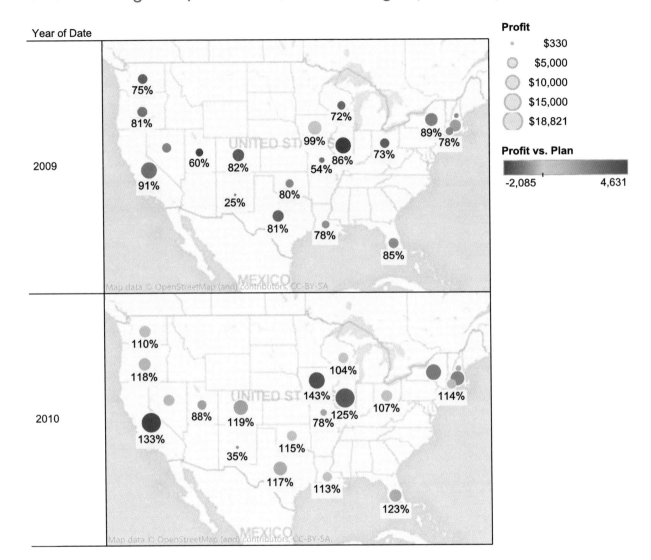

This map communicates a lot of information, thankfully mostly good news! Managers can quickly compare themselves with their peer states and all other states for both years. To easily interpret the features that you added to the map, look at one at a time:

- First, compare bubble sizes between states to see which states are bigger markets. Also, compare bubble sizes in 2009 with those in 2010 to see which states had bigger increases in profitability- for example, California and Illinois were strong profit growth states, which is great, since they also are larger markets.

- Look at the color-coding. Notice that in 2009 virtually the entire map is red, so planned profits were more than the actual profits (not good!), while in 2010 almost every state was green (good!). The more intense the red, the more inaccurate the plan, but keep in mind that these represent dollar amounts, so a dark red small bubble may not be as detrimental to the company's overall planned profits as a light red large bubble. Fortunately, the dark red bubbles in 2009 were in smaller markets (smaller bubbles) except for Illinois, which was darker green by 2010.

- The percentages tell you how inaccurate the plans were – the lower the percentage, the worse the performance of the state relative to plan. In addition to quantifying how off the plans were, these are different from just looking at the color coding because they are relative measurements, so you can compare smaller markets with larger markets. New Mexico was way off – profits totaled only 25% of the planned profits but Iowa almost reached the planned profits at 99%. 2010 was a completely new ball game- the vast majority of states met or exceeded their plans! In fact, the most profitable states vastly exceeded their plans by 20-40%.

View shifting- the underrated histogram and flexible bins

One of the product planners came to you and asked if she could give the regional sales managers a better understanding of the importance of lower volume items. She tells you that the higher volume products often get all the "love" and she wanted to see if her hunch was right, that the lower volume products are more important than commonly given credit.

After thinking about the best way to present this information, you realize an advanced form of a histogram (a bar chart that shows counts of items divided by category) would offer abundant insight into this question.

To meet this specific request, you will use a "Histogram" view with size- and color-coded values for profit. You will categorize sales into "bins" to create the histogram chart bars.

1. **Use <Ctrl>-M to add a New Worksheet.**

2. **Click on** *Sales* **in the Measures area and then click on Show Me!**. The Show Me! dialog will appear with the Aligned Bar graph type automatically selected by Tableau. **Change the view type to Histogram,** shown in Show Me! as single bar chart with a central peak. **Click OK**. A Histogram of *Sales* will appear with number of sales records automatically binned into intervals of 100: 0 to 99 is the 0 bar, 100 to 199 is the 100 bar, and so on.

Sales Histogram- understand the volume of orders by sale amount

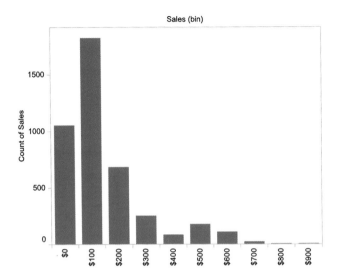

3. New Tableau users often want to know "what the dataset looks like" behind the view. To see the data in a more familiar spreadsheet form, **right-click on the view and select View data → Underlying** (we'll cover this feature more in a later chapter).

4. Note that with the data used in this sample, a count of sales records in each bin is not very useful. This is a simple summary of the number of monthly sales records for each item in each area code. To make this much more informative, change *CNT (Sales)* to *SUM (Sales)*. **Click on the down caret next to** *CNT (Sales)* **in the Row Shelf, select Measure (Count) and change the aggregate function to Sum.** The histogram is now considered an aligned bar chart by Tableau, so you will see this if you click on Show Me!. Technically, this is no longer a histogram because it no longer displays counts, but you used the histogram as a basis to describe the sales data.

   ! Alternate Route: You could have first binned the data and then used an aligned bar chart. Binning is covered in a later chapter.

5. Next, you want to differentiate between year and region. **Add** *Date* **to the Columns Shelf to the left of the** *Sales (bin)* **item already there and add** *Market* **to the Rows Shelf to the left of the** *Sum(Sales)* **data item.** Eight charts appear in the view – each of these will be referred to as a pane.

Sales Histogram by *Year* and *Market*

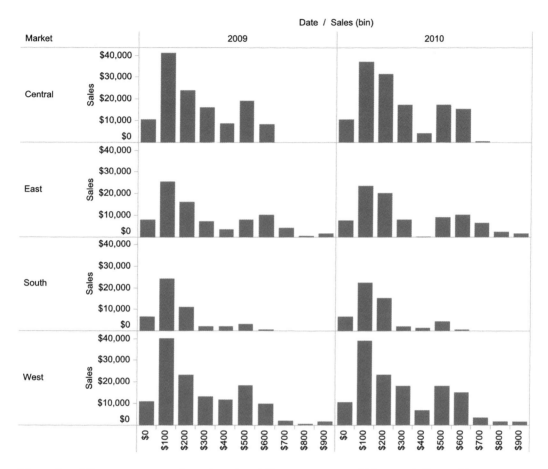

Note the different patterns found in the different regions. West and Central have pronounced peaks at $100 and $500, East and South have less pronounced peaks at $100 and East have more data at the upper end of the binned sales.

Next, you need to add profitability to contrast with sales. This can be accomplished by several simultaneous methods (similar to what you did above on the map): color-coding the bars, sizing the bars, and placing profit percentages above each bar.

6. **From the Measures area, add *Profit* three times to the Marks Card: Label, Color, and Size**.

7. You have to fix this up a little- the text is busy and detracts from the key purpose of the view. To better calculate the profit that is above each sales bin bar so that it is easier to understand, change it from sum of profit to percent of profit for that pane. **Click on the down caret next to *SUM (Profit)* in the Label shelf on the Marks Card and select Add Table Calculation from the dropdown.** The Table Calculation dialog appears.

The Table Calculation dialog

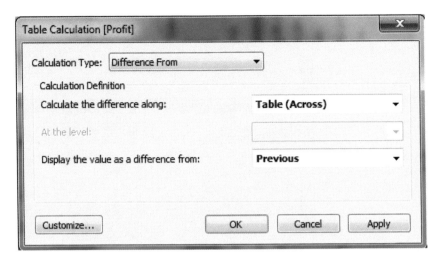

8. In the Table Calculation dialog, **change Calculation Type to Percent of Total,
    which changes the Calculation Definition options→ Under Calculation
    Definition→Summarize the values from→ select Pane from the drop down,
    and click OK.** The text values change to percentages in each view pane. These
    percentages are the percent of total profit for that pane in each binned sales bar. You
    notice that the default format is too precise for this purpose. **Right-click on** *SUM
    (Profit)* **in the Label box of the Marks Card, and select Format from the
    context menu.** The Format pane replaces the Data Items pane on the left side of the
    Tableau application. **Click on the dropdown by the Default Numbers selector, a
    dialog appears, select Percentage and change the Decimal places setting to
    "0". To close the Format Pane, click on the "x" at the upper right corner.**
    The Data Items pane reappears to the left of the view.

Sales Binned by *Year* and *Market, Profit* highlighted as percent of pane and encoded by both color and bar size

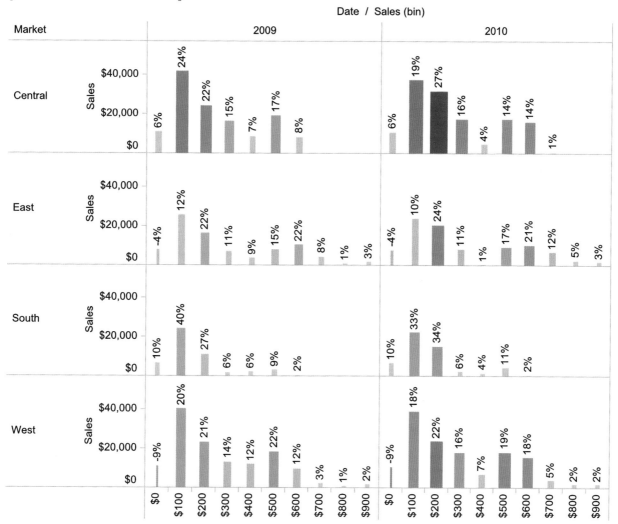

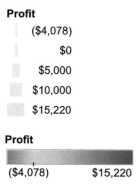

Profit

	($4,078)
	$0
	$5,000
	$10,000
	$15,220

Profit

($4,078) $15,220

You meet with the product planner to explain this insightful view. Some key insights stand out:

- Examining the binned monthly sales amounts on the horizontal axis, you can see that the highest revenue products are a relatively minor portion of the profits (profit percentage contribution is at top of each bar) across the entire company. For example, the East saw just 4%-8% of all profits generated by products generating revenue of $800-$1,000 per month.

- Examining the annual sales represented by bar heights, you can observe that products with the highest total sales rarely generate the greatest profitability, but they are typically very profitable nonetheless. For example, in the West in 2010, $100 per month products generated the greatest sales, but only 18% of profits, so they were not the highest profit makers in the pane. That would be products in the $200 bin (22%) followed by products in the $500 bin (19%). The South region is the exception: in 2009, the $100 bin generated the most profit (40%), and in 2010, the $100 bin (33%) was essentially tied for the highest profit with the $200 bin (34%).

- The East and West have pronounced profitability at the mid-sales volume product areas, with more than 34% to 40% of all profits being generated by these products, generating sales of $500-$700 per month.

- Another interesting point about this view is that the data in each pane exhibit a primary peak in annual sales at around $100 and a secondary peak at around $500. This also is known as a bimodal distribution.

Exporting results to share your insights

You have several options for distributing your results:

1) Sit down with the recipients and interactively explore the results and data via Tableau.

2) Install a copy of Tableau or a free Tableau Reader (downloadable from the Tableau website) for the recipients and share your Tableau project. Tableau has a server product built to make this sharing centralized and more manageable.

3) Export the results in the Tableau project via the Publish as PDF function, via **File → Print to PDF**.

   a. This is a very easy way to transfer Tableau results to people without Tableau.

   b. Unfortunately, unless you have purchased Adobe Acrobat (not just the free Reader version), you will not be able to edit and rearrange the results exported via this method.

4) Individually copy and paste views from Tableau to other applications, such as Microsoft PowerPoint and Word, via **Edit → Copy → Image or by right-clicking over the view and selecting Copy Image.**

   a. This is flexible and works across many Windows applications. The image is of high quality for general-purpose presentations. We frequently use this method throughout this book.

   b. Unfortunately, if you want to update a slide deck or Word document on a frequent basis, there is no automation method for this task, so you will need to copy it each time from Tableau.

5) Use the "dashboard" functionality in Tableau to combine multiple views created in a Tableau project into one unified "dashboard" view. Access this capability via **Edit → New Dashboard**.

Page intentionally left blank for proper book pagination

Chapter 4

Essential view types in Tableau

Chapter Highlights

- Understanding the core view categories in Tableau

    o   Text Tables- when the details are the point

    o   Heat Maps- how hot is it?

    o   Bar Charts- the most flexible views

Views are the foundation of Tableau, so mastering them is the key to optimizing your visualization insights. In this chapter, you will learn about the core view types.

In Tableau, you can use the "Show Me!" button to display the array of eighteen specific view types. Tableau automatically highlights the view that it "guesses" will be the most useful for the data items that you selected, and lets you know which other views are available. Views that are not appropriate due to the nature of your selected data items are grayed out on the Show Me! dialog.

If you accept the "Show Me!" view, you can easily change the view type later via "Show Me!" or by your own manual modifications to the shelves and settings. In fact, when you manually adjust your view, Tableau may surprise you by automatically changing it to the one wanted- that is the beauty of Tableau!

We have grouped the eighteen view templates into eight logical categories for your convenience. In this chapter, the first three view categories are covered: text tables, heat maps and bar charts. First, a summary table displays these three categories, which contain nine of the templates from Show Me!, along with a thumbnail picture and the data items required to use them as the basis of a view. Following the table, each view template is described, along with a simple example and the occasional advanced one.

View Category / Name	View Example	Required Dimension Items	Required Measure Items
Text Table- Text Table (Cross-Tab)		1 or more (may be 0 if have at least 1 measure)	1 or more (may be 0 if have at least 1 dimension)
Text Table- Highlight Table		1 or more	1 or more
Heat Map- Heat Map		1 or more	1 or 2
Bar Chart- Aligned Bar		0 or more	1 or more
Bar Chart- Stacked Bar		2 or more	1 or more
Bar Chart- Side-by-Side Bar		1 or more	2 or more
Bar Chart- Bar With Measure on Color		1 or more	2 or more
Bar Chart- Histogram		0 or more	1
Bar Chart- Bullet Graph		1 dimension	2 measures

Text Tables- an eye for detail

A Text Table is commonly referred to as a cross-tab or pivot table. It provides a way to display counts or measures relative to categorical variables. Tables are useful when it is important to look up individual data point values or when you want to compare them across one or more levels of dimensional detail.

1. *Text Table*- best choice when you require the ability to reference specific values for data precision and data checking. It is also the view that many Excel users are the most comfortable using. Text Tables are very flexible in Tableau and can easily morph into other view types, so if you want to review detailed data values before moving on to other view types, they are a good starting point.

    !Performance Tip: There is no need to add every field to the text table. Rather, start with a summary containing just a few crucial dimensions and then drill into the interesting areas by filtering and adding more detail when needed.

    ## A Text Table excerpt showing *Profit* and *Profit versus Plan* by *Market, Product, Year* and *Quarter*

| | | Profit | | | | | | | | Profit vs. Plan | | | | | | | |
| | | 2009 | | | | 2010 | | | | 2009 | | | | 2010 | | | |
Market	Product	Q1	Q2	Q3	Q4	Q1	Q2	Q3	Q4	Q1	Q2	Q3	Q4	Q1	Q2	Q3	Q4
Central	Amaretto	$497	$500	$556	$567	$659	$708	$755	$542	-182	-110	-134	-182	69	93	95	112
	Caffe Mocha	$1,419	$1,512	$1,607	$1,421	$2,128	$2,140	$2,271	$2,134	-811	-528	-562	-1,069	205	100	81	-276
	Chamomile	$1,422	$1,420	$1,515	$1,501	$2,162	$2,023	$2,142	$2,228	-127	-130	-105	-39	592	482	522	655
	Columbian	$542	$525	$515	$782	$1,271	$1,211	$1,287	$1,177	-227	-252	-255	-267	191	121	117	117
	Darjeeling	$1,050	$1,155	$1,220	$970	$1,552	$1,620	$1,722	$1,429	20	25	70	50	552	510	572	549
	Decaf Espre...	$250	$245	$274	$240	$1,422	$1,227	$1,235	$1,345	-420	-365	-405	-192	52	27	-45	-254
	Decaf Irish C...	$205	$1,045	$1,059	$552	$1,270	$1,475	$1,505	$1,223	-222	-273	-251	-291	340	158	195	142
	Earl Grey	$291	$1,073	$1,072	$1,070	$1,495	$1,520	$1,515	$1,592	51	55	62	180	595	500	505	702
	Green Tea	$77	$97	$120	$205	$117	$122	$154	$205	-12	-2	-10	-5	27	22	44	95
	Lemon	$552	$719	$677	$274	$579	$1,016	$252	$554	-195	-151	-192	-178	99	116	52	104
	Mint	$299	$420	$455	$275	$501	$505	$542	$557	-21	-40	-34	-25	151	135	153	157
East	Amaretto	$74	$109	$120	$100	$111	$154	$182	$149	-35	-21	-50	-50	1	24	-7	-1
	Caffe Mocha	($555)	($524)	($552)	($521)	($554)	($554)	($527)	($527)	-225	-254	-259	-291	-534	-514	-577	-597
	Chamomile	$102	$101	$75	$33	$155	$142	$105	$49	13	11	5	-17	65	52	35	-1
	Columbian	$2,461	$2,940	$2,295	$2,420	$2,714	$4,150	$4,555	$2,657	-59	-110	-142	20	1,154	1,100	1,215	1,197
	Darjeeling	$545	$575	$710	$515	$572	$557	$1,002	$919	-195	-154	-210	-152	123	97	52	119

An excerpt of the same Text Table

filtered and color-encoded by *Product Type*

Market	Product Type	Product	Date					Product Type
			Profit		Profit vs. Plan			■ Coffee
			2009		2009			■ Espresso
			Q1	Q2	Q1	Q2		■ Herbal Tea
Central	Coffee	Amaretto	$457	$500	-163	-110		■ Tea
		Columbian	$843	$928	-237	-252		
		Decaf Irish Cream	$908	$1,045	-222	-275		
	Espresso	Caffe Mocha	$1,419	$1,512	-511	-528		
		Decaf Espresso	$950	$945	-430	-365		
	Herbal Tea	Chamomile	$1,433	$1,430	-137	-130		
		Lemon	$582	$719	-198	-181		
		Mint	$399	$430	-21	-40		
	Tea	Darjeeling	$1,050	$1,155	20	35		
		Earl Grey	$991	$1,075	81	55		
		Green Tea	$77	$87	-13	-3		

2. *Highlight Table*- useful for emphasizing the range of values in a table by using color, while still allowing easy access to the detailed values. In the following table, notice how quickly you can see that 2009 was much less profitable relative to plan than 2010. Coffee was the worst relative performer in both years, and Tea was the best relative performer in both years.

A Highlight Table showing *Profit as a % of Plan* by *Product Type*
for *Year* and *Quarter*

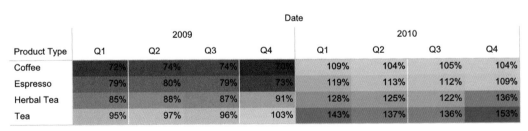

	Date							
	2009				2010			
Product Type	Q1	Q2	Q3	Q4	Q1	Q2	Q3	Q4
Coffee	72%	74%	74%	70%	109%	104%	105%	104%
Espresso	79%	80%	79%	73%	119%	113%	112%	109%
Herbal Tea	85%	88%	87%	91%	128%	125%	122%	136%
Tea	95%	97%	96%	103%	143%	137%	136%	153%

Profit as a % of Plan

70%   153%

Heat Maps- how intense is it?

Heat Maps enable easy comparison of categorical values using color ranges. Use these when the specific values are less important than quickly identifying the trends based on the intensity or "temperature" of a measure, or when you have many members in several dimensions (e.g., all product sales and profits in all zip codes). The layout is similar to a text table with variations in values encoded as colors.

A Heat Map showing *Profit as a % of Plan* (color-encoded) and *Sales* (size-encoded) by *Product* and *Market* for *Year* and *Quarter*

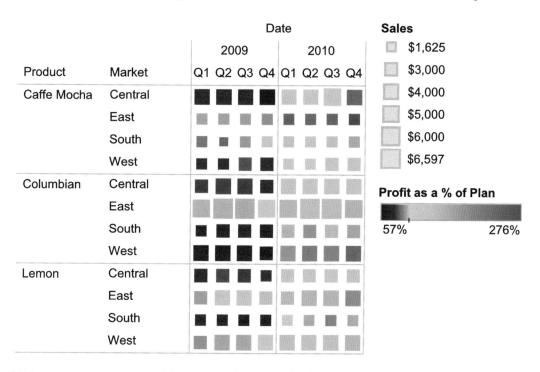

In this heat map, you can quickly see a wide array of information. East is the biggest seller of Columbian (size of square). Caffe Mocha in the East was the only product to hit the profit plan target throughout 2009 (all green squares). Central is the biggest seller of Caffe Mocha (also size of square). West and South have significantly below profit plan products in 2010 (red squares).

Bar Charts- six flavors to meet your needs

Bar Charts are the most flexible of the chart types and can be used for almost any visual analysis that involves categories or dimensions but does not require a text table- from dimensional comparisons to data ranking to data distribution to time series. As a bonus, bar charts are also very easy to digest since the human visual system is quite effective at understanding and rapidly comparing bar lengths.

Since bar charts encode the data values by the length of the bar, bar charts have one key constraint: Tableau must show the zero value on your measure axis or the analysis will be misleading. Fortunately, this occurs automatically in Tableau.

1. *Aligned Bar*- useful for comparing two or more measures across a dimension. The overall shape and trend of the bars can be compared, even when multiple measures are used on different scales or units of measure.

An Aligned Bar Chart for key US economic and tax measures by year, 1968-2007

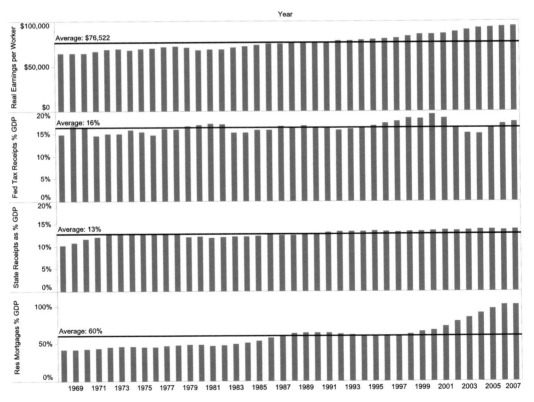

The sample aligned bar chart explores US economic data over 40 years, from 1968-2007. Beginning at the top of the view, the four measures shown are *Real Earnings per Worker* (adjusted to 2007 dollars), *Federal Tax Receipts as a Percent of GDP*, *State Tax Receipts as a Percent of GDP* and *Residential Mortgages (Outstanding) as a Percent of GDP*. A reference line has been added to each pane to represent the average of the pane across the 40- year period, allowing quick comparison within each pane relative to the overall measure average.

Key observations from this complex aligned bar view:

- The increase in *Real Earnings per Worker* is very impressive over the 40-year period.

- *Federal Tax Receipts as a Percent of GDP* has varied over the period, but not by more than a few percent less or more than the average.

- *State Tax Receipts as a Percent of GDP* also has varied, but appear to have increased more consistently than *Federal Tax Receipts as a Percent of GDP*.

- *Residential Mortgages as a Percent of GDP* has grown in spurts with radical growth in the last 8 years, driving them way above the historic average.

- *Federal versus State Tax Receipts as a Percent of GDP* are closer than popular perception, an average of 16% versus just 3% of GDP less for state receipts at 13%.

- The biggest concern after examining this view is the radical growth in *Residential Mortgages as a Percent of GDP*. Perhaps lower interest rates could temper this growth, but this definitely warrants further research.

2. <u>Stacked Bar</u>- good for showing overall trend across categories or over time while simultaneously comparing the trend within categories for absolute measures. If you have an aligned bar chart with have many categories that requiring extensive scrolling to review, a stacked bar chart can be a good alternative.

A Stacked Bar Chart of *Profit* by *Quarter* and *Market*

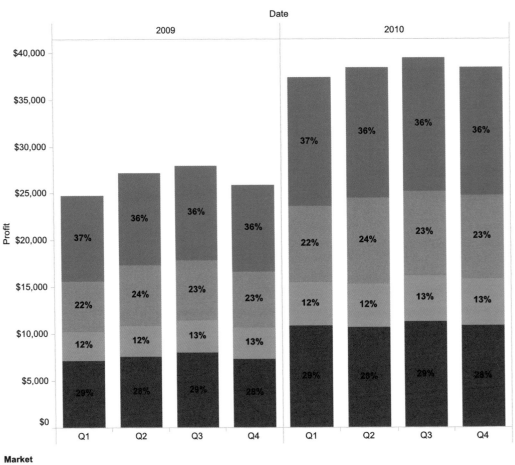

3. *Side-by-Side Bar*- while aligned bars are generally superior, side-by-side bar charts can be useful when comparing similar measures within each cell.

A Side-by-Side Bar Chart of *Profit* and *Profit versus Plan* by *Year* and *Product Type*

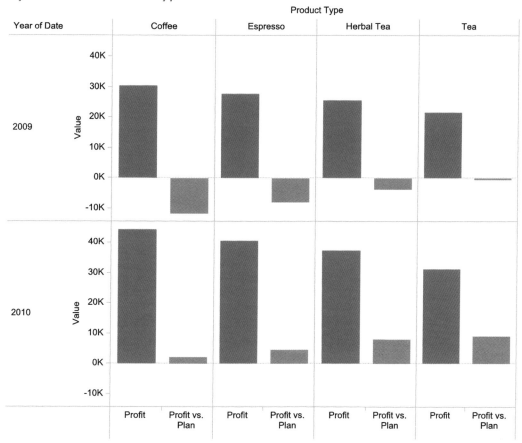

Measure Names
- Profit
- Profit vs. Plan

4. *Bar with Measure on Color*- another alternative to the aligned bar chart. In addition to the related primary measure (bar length), color encoding can be useful for understanding intensity of a measure, as shown in the following view.

A Bar Chart with Measure on Color

Marketing spend by Product and Region, 2009 and 2010; with *Profit versus Plan* in color and shown as labels

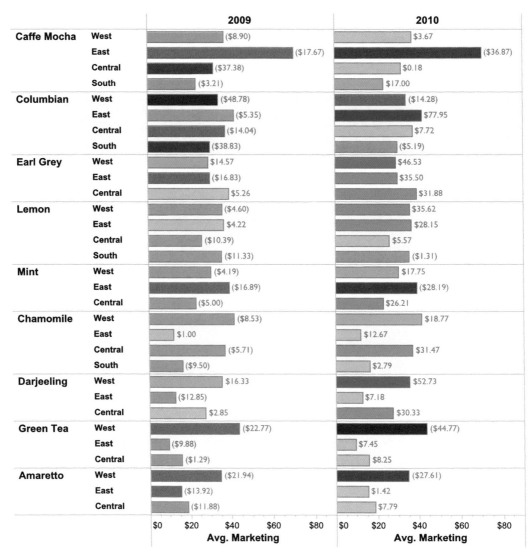

Avg. Profit vs Plan

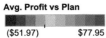

($51.97) $77.95

5. _Histogram_- a specialized bar chart that displays frequencies of a value or range of values. By convention, these are usually vertical (up and down) bars. A histogram is useful for examining the distribution of occurrences.

A Histogram showing annual unemployment rates, 1968-2007

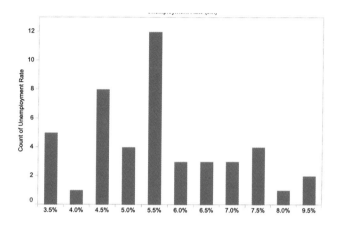

An enhanced histogram with Trend Line-
annual unemployment rates by presidential party, 1968-2007

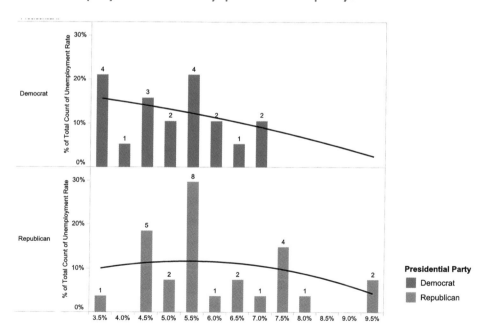

6. <u>*Bullet Graph*</u>- an alternative to using dashboard gauges or meters to indicate how close you have come to attaining a goal. This is a cutting-edge graph type developed by Stephen Few at UC-Berkeley. It displays a lot of information in a compact area, yet it is easy to read (once you understand how it works). You can use bullet graphs if you have a dimension and two related measures- an actual measure, such as *Profit*, and a target measure, such as *Budget Profit*.

A Bullet Graph with *Profit* by *State- Budget Profit* as the target

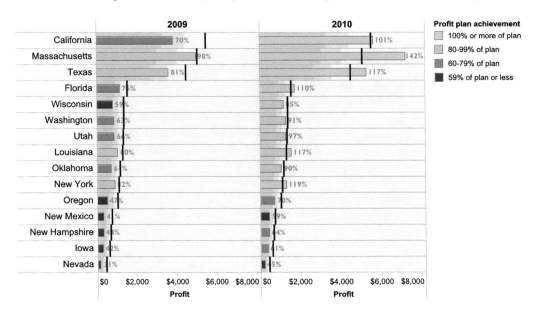

The horizontal bar is the "bullet", *Profit* in this example, shown by *State*. The small, black vertical line is the "target", *Budget Profit* in this example, the planned profit for each state by year. This graph is sorted in descending order by *Budget Profit*, to emphasize the state with the highest targets. The bars are color-encoded, depending upon how close each state's actual profit is to the planned profit. Note that none of the states achieved their target in 2009 but several achieved their goal in 2010!

One last element of the bullet graph is for quick reference- the area behind the bars shaded in dark gray indicates 0-60% of the target, the range from the dark gray to the mid-gray areas indicates 60-80% of the target and the light gray area is 80% and above the target.

! *Performance Tip*: Since Tableau is unaware of whether a particular measure is a target or an actual value, it may place the items in the wrong position for your Bullet Graph. The target should appear on the Level of Detail shelf. If you need to swap the measures, right-click on the horizontal axis and select Swap Reference Line Fields. If you attempt to swap them by manually dragging and dropping the fields, you will lose key elements of the Bullet Graph, which you will need to add back manually!

Chapter 5

Advanced view types in Tableau

Chapter Highlights

- Understanding the five advanced view categories in Tableau

  - Line Charts- once upon a time

  - Scatter Plots- do they move together?

  - Gantt Chart- time after time

  - Pie Chart- a surprise that may please some

  - Maps (Geographic)- what happened where?

- Combination charts- overlay multiple chart types

Views are the foundation of Tableau, so mastering them is the key to optimizing your visualization insights. In the last chapter, you learned about the basic view types. This chapter explains the advanced view types. Additionally, we include combination charts at the end, in which you can overlay different view types by customizing marks for different measures.

In Tableau, you can use the "Show Me!" button to display the array of eighteen specific view types. Tableau automatically highlights the view that it "guesses" will be most useful for the data items that you selected, and lets you know which other views are available. Views that are not appropriate due to the nature of your selected data items are grayed out on the Show Me! dialog.

If you accept the "Show Me!" view, you can easily change the view type later via "Show Me!" or by your own manual modifications to the shelves and settings.

We have grouped the eighteen view templates into eight logical categories for your convenience. In this chapter, the remaining five view categories are covered (along with combination charts). First, a summary table displays these five categories, which contain nine of the templates from Show Me!, along with a thumbnail picture and the data items required to use them as the basis of a view. Following the table, each view template is described, along with examples.

View Category / Name	View Example	Required Dimension Items	Required Measure Items
Line Chart- Line (Discrete)		1 date	1 or more
Line Chart- Line (Continuous)		1 date or continuous dimension	1 or more
Scatter Plot- Circle		1 or more	1 or more
Scatter Plot- Scatter (Single)		0 or more	2 to 4
Scatter Plot- Scatter (Matrix)		1 or more categorical	3 to 6
Scatter Plot- Dual Axis		1 or more	2 or more
Gantt Chart- Gantt		1 plus 1 continuous dimension or date	0
Pie Chart- Pie		1 or more	1 or more
Map- Map		1 geographic dimension plus 0 or more	1 or more

Line Charts- describe what happened recently

When a dimension field includes a date, "Show Me!" recommends a line chart because it is more effective than a bar chart for showing trends across multiple categories. The default is to treat the date dimension as a discrete variable, meaning that the next highest level of date data is used to break the lines into regions in the chart (see the 1st example below). Note that the default date view is shown at the year level of detail. If you drill down to quarter, the view is broken into regions by year.

1. *Line (Discrete)* - useful for showing trends over time across one or more categories. Notice in the example that 2009 and 2010 have different patterns for Regular coffee profits in addition to being higher overall year over year. By making the chart discrete in the view, it is easy to compare quarters across the year- Q3 in 2010 is very different for Regular coffee but similar for Decaf.

A Discrete Line Chart of *Profit* by *Month* for 2009-2010,
with *Coffee Type* in color

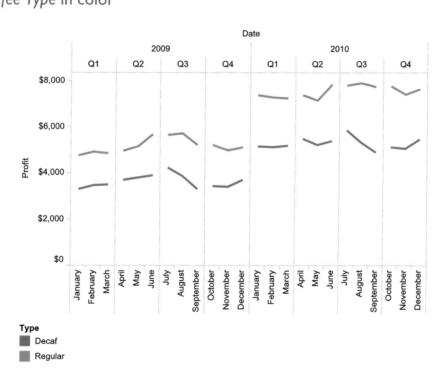

2. <u>*Line (Continuous)*</u> **-** Continuous line charts are useful at exploring the relationship of two continuous measures as shown below. While date data items can be used with this chart type, it is recommended to use a discrete line chart instead of a continuous line chart.

The example below clearly shows a very different product margin pattern for items shipped via delivery truck than via the other two modes, especially at the higher margin levels. Regular air shipments have a very pronounced peak at lower margin levels while the other two modes have less pronounced peaks in this range of margin. Note that the scales of the axes for the three different ship modes are not all the same- this was changed to compare the overall shape of the lines rather than specific values.

A Continuous Line Chart showing *Sales* by *Product Base Margin* categorized by *Ship Mode*

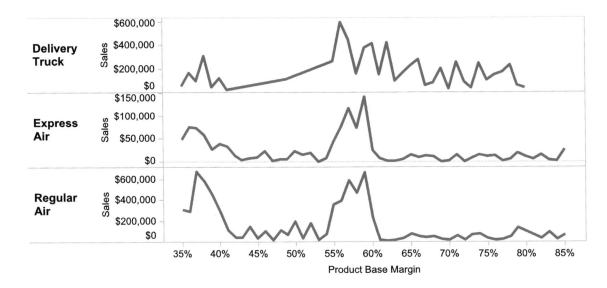

Scatter Plots- relationships matter

Scatter plots are very useful for understanding the relationship of one or more measures, often referred to as correlation. Scatter plots are very effective for comparing one or more measures and how the other measures vary across each measure and/or category. Tableau offers four distinct types of scatter plots: Circle, Scatter (Single), Scatter (Matrix) and Dual Axis.

1. *Circle*- the simplest form of scatter plot, highlighted by Show Me! when you select one or more dimensional items *that are not date- or location-related* and one measure. The example shown here does an excellent job of highlighting that furniture and office supplies provide nearly identical average profits for the company, while the average profit of technology products is about four times higher. The average profit overall for all product categories combined (grand total) and for office supplies alone is very tightly clustered around their average for all four segments. Meanwhile, for furniture and technology, average profit covers a larger range across the four segments, with furniture being more profitable for the consumer and home office segments, and technology for corporate and small business customers.

A Circle Scatter Plot of *Average Profit* by *Product Category*
with *Customer Segment* in color

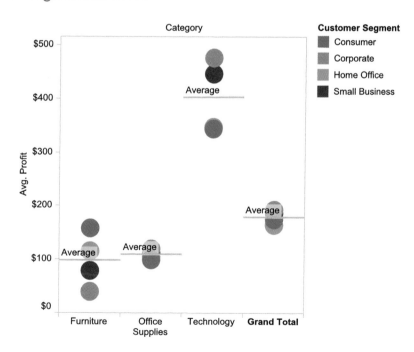

2. <u>*Scatter (Single)*</u> - compares two or more measures and at least one dimension. The example contains a rich amount of information. The highest selling product/order priority combinations are not always the most profitable ones. Critical shipments often take more time to ship than lower priority shipments (not good). Also, it appears that Critical shipments are quite different in the East region. Perhaps there are a higher percentage of order errors in this category resulting in critical priority "fixes", indicating a potential company issue for this region.

A Single Scatter Plot of *Average Profit* by *Sales* across *Region-*
Average Time to Ship Size-encoded and *Order Priority* Color-encoded

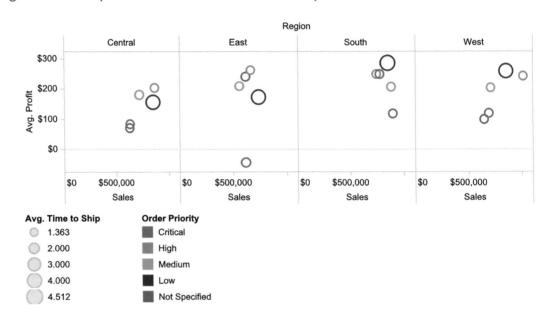

3. _Scatter (Matrix)_ - useful for comparing several measures against one another. All measures are placed on a "grid" (matrix) of multiple scatter plots- every measure is shown against every other measure (including itself) to allow simultaneous viewing of multiple relationships. Each measure can be examined across either the horizontal axis (also known as the X-axis) or the vertical axis (also known as the Y-axis) against every other measure.

In Tableau 6, selecting a point highlights it in all the other scatter plots, which makes it simple to see how an outlier in one plot performs in the other plots. Therefore, you can look at the inverted data, which is useful for examining the relationships from two perspectives visually. Additionally, to understand the impact of categorical data across the plots, one or more dimensions may be encoded in the plots using color or shape.

The example that follows compares various consumer price indices (CPI) by year. The years are also color-encoded by decade.

A Matrix Scatter Plot of three parts of the Consumer Price Index-
decade of occurrence is color-encoded

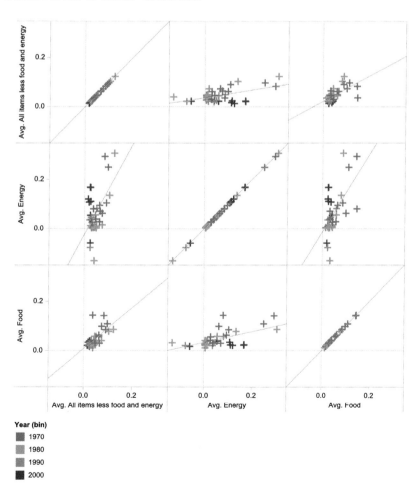

The three measures are *All items less food and energy* (located at the top on the vertical axis and the left on horizontal axis), *Energy* (the middle on both axes) and *Food* (the bottom on the vertical axis and the right on the horizontal axis).

Starting in the bottom middle plot, you can see that in years when the *Energy* CPI is higher, the *Food* CPI is also higher. The trend line shows an approximate relationship, with the growth rate of food prices being higher in high-energy price years, but the rate of growth is slower than energy prices, by about half.

Moving just one plot to the left, you can see that as *All items less food and energy* move up, that *Food* prices move up almost in unison. There are two years that are outliers, 1973 and 1974 (if this graph was in Tableau right now, you could see the specific year by hovering the cursor over the data points in the view.) Examining the same information inverted in the upper right plot shows that there might be a more complex shape to this relationship, which may be worth further investigation and analysis.

Finally, moving to the second row and first column, you can see that *All items less food and energy* have a nearly vertical relationship with energy price changes. There does appear to be a number of years with some linear pattern but also a number of outlier years in multiple decades. This warrants further research before reaching conclusions about whether or not a relationship exists.

4. _Dual Axis_- useful for examining two or more related measures in the same view space or two or more relevant measures that have different units of measurement (e.g., dollars sold and units sold.) Using shape and/or color encoding, the different measurements can be displayed in the same view area, enabling easy comparison of multiple measures.

The example below contrasts e-mail and printed newsletter sales for a winery over 24 months. For each month, _E-mail Sales_ is color-encoded as blue and scaled to the left axis, while _Newsletter Sales_ is orange and scaled to the right axis.

A Dual Axis line chart of E-mail versus Newsletter sales

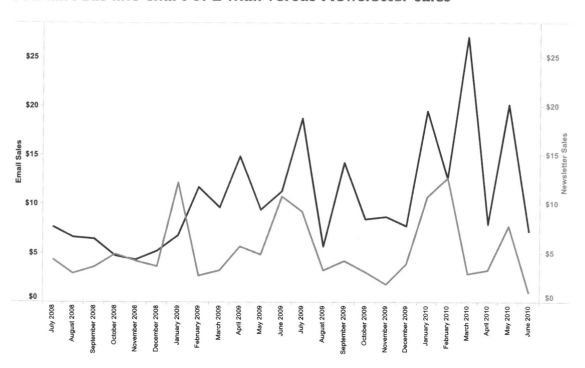

With some modest modifications, even more information can be obtained from this chart. By adding a pane subdivision of the two years by Fiscal Year and adding average reference lines for e-mail and newsletter sales in each year, you can see that e-mail sales are growing aggressively while overall newsletter sales are flat over the two years. Additionally, the monthly variability of both e-mail and newsletter sales appears to be increasing over the two-year period.

By adding panes for each fiscal year and average reference lines,
further insights are immediately available from these data

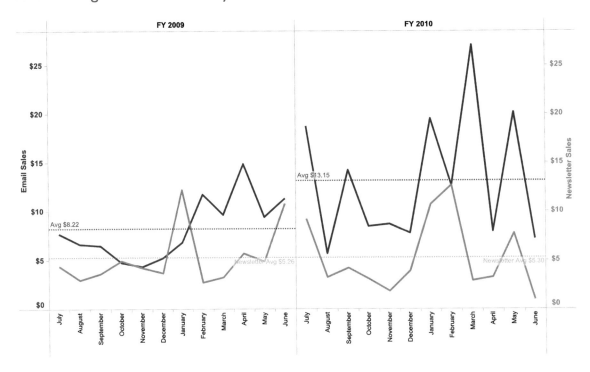

Gantt Chart- understand the details over time

Gantt charts are a specialized type of chart that can be very useful at showing events repeated over time or a range of another continuous dimension. Creating these for the first time can be confusing if you use the Show Me! button. Show Me! restricts the Column axis (horizontal or X-axis) to continuous dimension items and the Row axis (vertical or Y-axis) to discrete dimension items- neither can be a measure item!

The example that follows is a slightly modified Gantt chart (in a classic Gantt chart, the bars would be varying widths to represent a second time dimension, such as "time to delivery" placed on the size shelf). This chart displays *Time to Ship* for various orders in a company. The *Ship Date* of each shipment is shown in the chart and the *Ship mode* is color-encoded. The rows of the chart along the Y-axis show the number of days required for the shipment to arrive at the customer **relative to the date the order was received.**

A Gantt Chart of time to ship in the South region,
April 2008 – March 2009

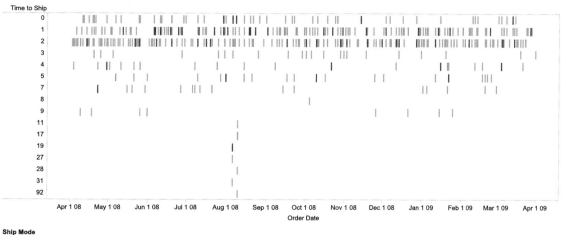

Examining this chart yields great insight into troubled shipments, taking up to 92 days to arrive. By backtracking from the arrival dates, you can determine that most of these were ordered in August of 2008. The three slowest shipments were all sent via Regular Air.

Pie Charts- by popular demand

Tableau having a Pie Chart view is akin to chickens having a pet hawk- much unexpected! Tableau likely added this view type due to popular customer demand, in spite of the well-known minimal utility of this view type. Both Edward Tufte and Stephen Few (highly respected experts in data visualization) rail against the overuse of this chart type and with good cause- they are frequently misleading and inappropriate for effectively conveying information. Unfortunately, they are popular in business applications due to earlier graphics programs that emphasized this chart type due to their "appetite" appeal- after all, who doesn't like pie? The easiest fallback from a pie chart habit is a bar chart, which is typically superior at conveying the information in your data.

A good rule to remember when using pie charts is to limit the number of slices shown to five or less. If you have more than five slices, you should use the grouping capability of Tableau to reduce the less important slices past the top four into one "Other" slice. Another serious issue with pie charts is the fact that measures with negative values, averages, minimums, maximums, etc. will be very misleading in the slices- so avoid them at all costs if you have measures with negative values (like profitability, shown below to illustrate the issue at the pie size level.)

Given the limitations, the example below shows a relatively useful application of pie charts, but one that is rarely used. The example shows *Profit* of an office equipment firm across *Region*, *Product Category*, and *Customer Segment*- with the overall size of the pie conveying the overall profit level at the intersection of *Region* and *Product Category*. Additional clarity is added by sorting all three dimension items by descending sum of profit.

A grid of Pie Charts showing *Profit* (overall pie size)
by *Region, Product,* and *Customer Segment*

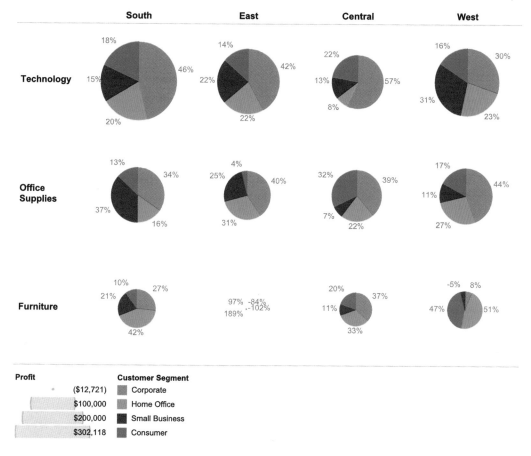

It is easy to see that the South region has the most profitable product line with technology products, since it is the largest pie, and that corporate customers are the most profitable in every region/product intersection, as the orange corporate "slices" are always the largest.

One oddity is the fact that the East/furniture intersection has negative profitability! How can a pie be a negative size since the area of the pie conveys the relative contribution of the pie? Tableau attempts to overcome this deficiency of pie charts by making the pie nearly invisible, which is a good compromise if you must use pie charts, but the best solution would be to use a different view type, such as bar charts.

Geographic Maps- what happened where?

Maps with size- or color-encoded shapes are available if your dataset has country, state, or postal code level data available. These are particularly useful if you want to convey the spatial distribution of one or more measures. You can also display the measures over various dimension categories across multiple views of the map.

The sample map shows social insurance data from 2006 for the United States divided by state. The two metrics displayed are *Social insurance paid to the residents of a state* divided by *Social insurance paid by the residents of a state* (size-encoded) and the *Social insurance dollar amount paid out per person in the state* (color-encoded).

Federal government social insurance payout in 2006
as a *Percent of Social Insurance Paid* (Square Size)
and *Total Dollars Spent per Person* (Color-Encoded)

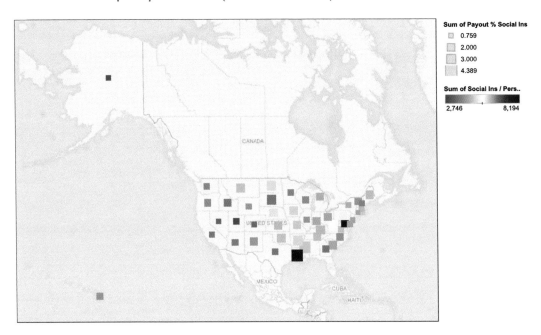

Examining this map yields some interesting regional information- the red squares identify which states have a high proportion of net inflows from federal social insurance programs. Louisiana is the highest on the payout scale relative to dollars paid into social insurance programs, probably due to Hurricane Katrina in 2005. Additionally, Mississippi and the Dakotas have high payout ratios. Looking at the square size, you can see that these same states also have large absolute dollar inflows per person, but so does the District of Columbia, one addition to the former list. Effectively, this map shows net subsidies from wealthier states to generally less wealthy states.

Combination charts: overlaying multiple charts

Combination charts allow you to combine multiple mark types in one view. You can do this by customizing the marks differently for different measures by right-clicking on the axis for the measure. We have included two examples to demonstrate what is possible in Tableau.

The first example is a Pareto chart, which contains both a bar graph and a line graph. The bars are in descending order from left to right, and the line chart depicts the cumulative total of the bars, increasing from left to right. This chart depicts proven oil reserves by country on the bar chart, and cumulative running total of the percentage of the world's oil that is found in those countries.

Combination chart: Pareto chart of world oil reserves

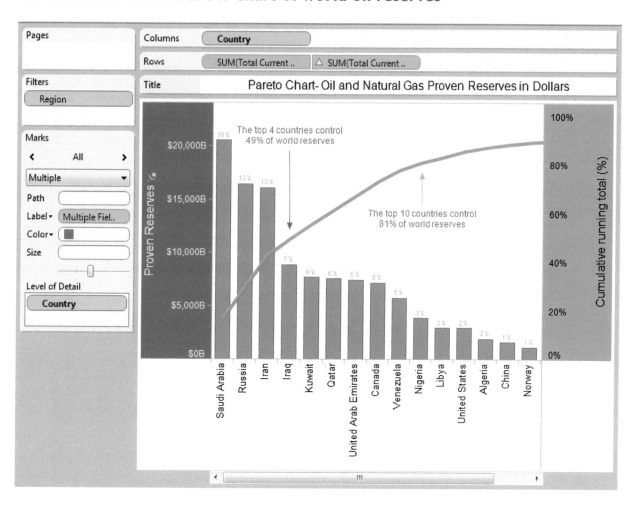

The second combination chart is made of a Line (Discrete) Chart and a Circle plot. The line represents quarterly average search volume for mortgage loans, and the circles show daily values in the same quarter.

Combination chart: Mortgage loan search volume on Google

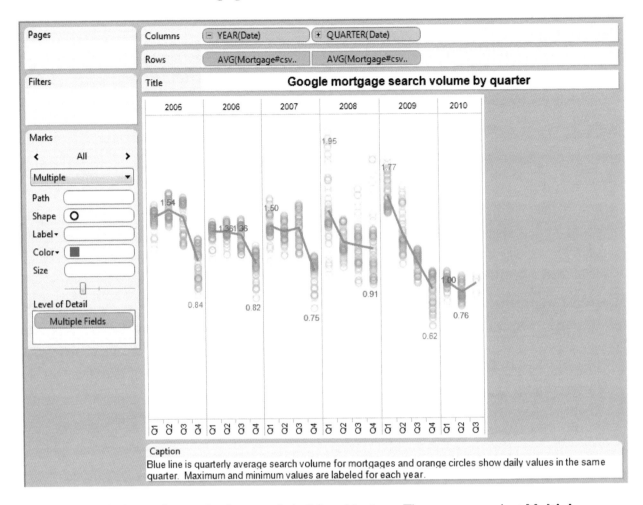

Assembling a dual-axis chart is the first step in building this view. Then, you can select **Multiple Mark Types** from the drop-down menu at the upper right of the Marks card. When you activate this feature, you will see a new selector for "All" marks, and a selection for mark in particular. For example, the above Google Mortgage volume example has a mark type of Multiple shown when All is selected, Line when the first average Mortgage volume item is selected, and Shape when the second Mortgage Volume is selected. Additionally, the second mortgage Mark selection has MDY(Date) added to the Level of Detail shelf, which forces the chart to show a daily value in orange.

Activating the Multiple Mark Types
and the new Marks Card appearance once activated

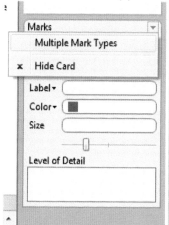 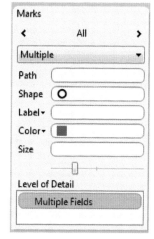

By using the left and right arrow tip pointers, you can scroll
through the multiple metrics used in your view and customize their appearance

 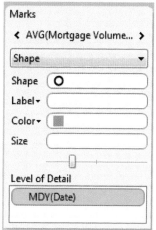

Page intentionally left blank for proper book pagination

Chapter 6

Taking over with Tableau - View structure, Marks Card, Summaries, Formatting and Titles

---

Chapter Highlights

- Customizing views using the Columns, Rows, Pages and Filters shelves

- Enhance your visual appeal with the Marks Card

- The Summary Card- rapid data insights

- Headers and axes

- Titles, captions, field labels, legends

- Formatting values in your views

This chapter reviews many of the capabilities of Tableau that take you beyond the powerful Show Me! defaults and empower you to customize and even build your own views from scratch.

This chapter uses the **Sample Coffee Chain dataset**. When you're prompted to return to the default view, **select the following three data items by keeping the <Ctrl> key depressed:** *Market*, *Product Type* and *Profit*. **Click Show Me! and keep the default selection, Aligned Bar Chart, by clicking OK**.

Default view: Aligned Bar Chart

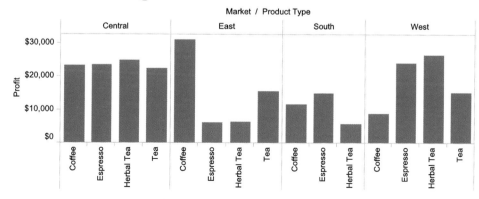

Customizing Views from Columns, Rows, Pages and Filters Shelves

In this section, you will learn to manually create or modify views via the Columns, Rows, Pages, and Filters shelves, which are located underneath the toolbar to the right of the Data Items pane.

1. <u>*Columns*</u>: when you place data items on the Columns shelf, such as *Market* and *Product Type* in the default view, you create the vertical column aspect of the view. These data items subdivide the view into vertical columns by determining which values are included on the X-axis (horizontal axis). Starting with the default view, **drag and drop** *Date* **to the right of** *Product Type* **in the Columns shelf.** The chart type automatically changes from Aligned Bar to Line (Discrete).

! *Alternate Route*: Move the *Date* field to the first position on the Columns shelf to see a different view of the data. Tableau is all about discovery, so feel free to experiment and move data items around in the examples to see how the insights change!

Modifying the view by placing *Date* on the Columns shelf

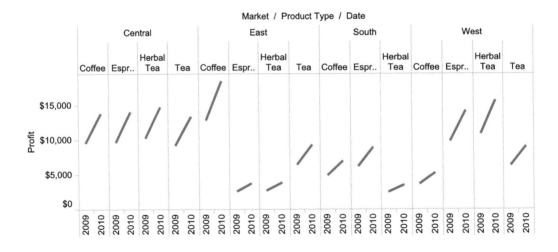

2. <u>Rows</u>: determines the values shown horizontally across the rows of the view. Using the Rows shelf, you can partition your chart into horizontal groups by choosing what is included on the Y-axis (vertical axis). **Add** *Market Size* **to the left of** *SUM(Profit)* **on the Rows shelf.**

Modifying the view by placing *Market Size* on the Rows shelf

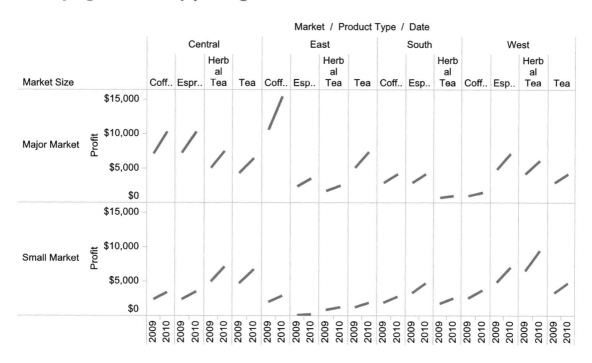

3. <u>Pages</u>: if you add a data item to the Pages shelf, you subset the complete view that displays all of the values of that data item into multiple views available on different "pages". The Pages feature allows you to scroll through the various page item values or across time. When you export or print the view, it will only display the currently selected page (similar to a filter, except that the number of rows and columns does not change across pages).

Add *Type* **to the Pages shelf**. Underneath the Pages shelf, the Current Page Card appears, with Decaf displayed in both the drop-down menu and the view. If you click the down carat next to Decaf, you can see that the other available *Type* is Regular. You can change to the Regular view in four ways: **by choosing Regular from the drop-down menu, clicking on the arrow directly to the right, moving the arrow on the progress bar in the middle of the card to the right, or using the scroll bar found on the bottom left of the card.** The three buttons found on the bottom right of the card are used to adjust the speed at which the view changes between Decaf and Regular, in case you would like to make visual comparisons between the two.

Data item *Type* on the Pages shelf, page controls below data item

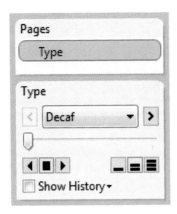

Modifying the view by placing *Type* on the Pages shelf-
Decaf page shown

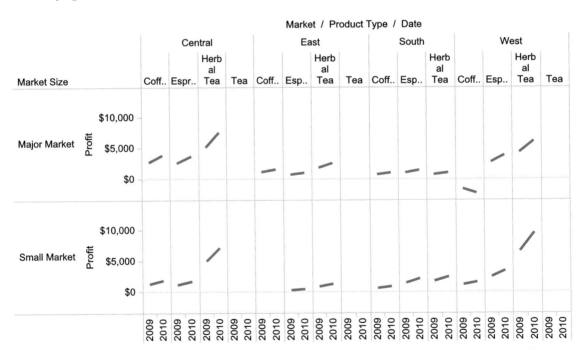

In contrast with the Filter shelf, placing items on the Pages shelf forces Tableau to examine the data for all available headers across all pages and the full range of axis values for every item in the page selection list. Tableau then forces all views to display every header and the full axis range on each page without regard for the current items header and axis range values. The intent is to allow you to visually examine for gaps and variability amongst the various items as you interact with this shelf.

4. _Filters_: using the filters shelf can help you focus on what you need and potentially decrease query times by reducing both the data aggregated and retrieved from the data source and the data displayed in the view. For instance, you may only want to look at particular dates, products, or locations and exclude others from the current view. **Add** _Product_ **to the Filters shelf.**

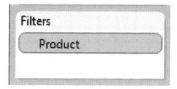

A dialog box will pop up- from the General tab, change the setting from "Select from List" to "Use All" (you could manually specify which products to further filter here, but we want the top 3 overall), then click on the tab labeled Top, select By Field → Top → 3 → Profit → Sum → OK.

Advanced features of the Filter dialog

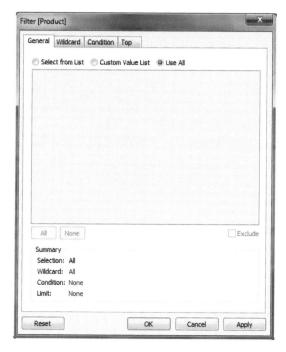
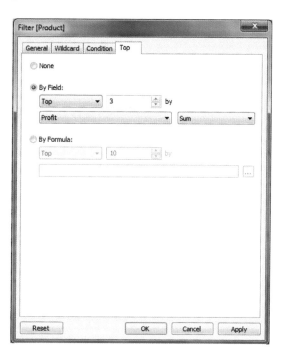

Modifying the view by placing *Product* on the Filters shelf

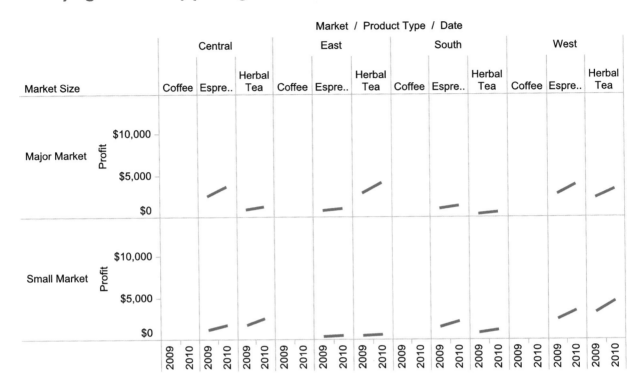

It is important to note that the Filter dialog has a General tab and three additional tabs that interact with the General tab in a specific manner. Item selection in the General tab affects the other tabs results. For example, if you select Lemon tea and Espresso from the General tab and then request the Top 3 items by Sum of Profit, you will only see two products returned since you only selected two items in the General tab.

Additionally, if you selected all products with the tick marks in the General tab and then choose the Top tab for ranking, Tableau will automatically select Use All on the General tab. This is to ensure that all products are automatically included in your Top/Bottom rankings. If you prefer to first select a subset of products and then select a subset of them based on rank, you can return to the first tab and select individual items once you have turned on the Top tab functionality.

Enhance visual appeal with the Marks card

As shown in previous chapters, the Marks card has a variety of functions that help you build exactly the right view. A mark represents a row (or aggregated group of rows) from your original data source. With the Marks card, you can design the appearance of these marks by placing data items on the Text, Label, Path, Color, Size, Shape and Level of Detail shelves. Note that the Text, Label, Path and Shape shelf are specific to certain view types, so you won't always see them on the Marks card.

Please reset your view to the default layout shown at the beginning of this chapter by selecting *Market*, *Product Type* **and** *Profit*, **clicking Show Me!, and then clicking OK. Then place** *Market* **on the Filters shelf. When the dialog box pops up, uncheck South and click OK.** This removes South from the view and retains Central, East and West.

! *Alternate Route*: Right-click on South and select Exclude. Alternatively, click on *Market* on the Columns shelf, select Show Quick Filter and uncheck South on the *Market* filter card that appears on the right side of the view.

1. *Label*: For graphs such as bar charts and maps, the dropdown to the right of the data item on the Label shelf allows you to select which type of aggregate value, such as sum, average, count, etc., that you would like to represent a specific variable or metric to summarize data items in charts. The basic use of the label feature is to highlight the same variable or metric with different aggregate values. Also, you can change mark label settings, such as font, by using the dropdown directly to the right of the word "Label".

   Add *Profit* **to the Label shelf. Click on the down carat to the right of** *Profit* **in the Label shelf, scroll down to Measure (Sum) and change the aggregate function from Sum to Average.**

Modifying the view by placing *Profit* on the Label shelf and

changing the aggregate function to Average

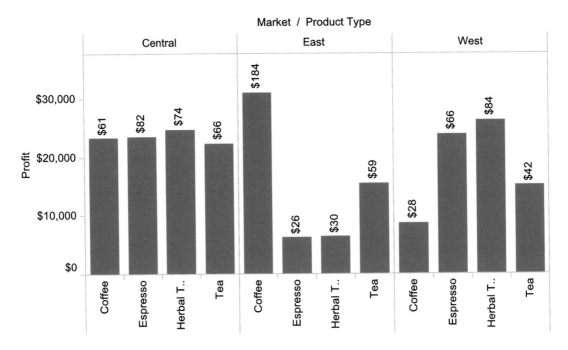

2. Text: this is very similar to Label, except that it is displayed in place of Label on the Marks Card when your view is a table or cross tab instead of a graph. The dropdown to the right of the data item allows you to select which type of aggregate value that you would like to represent a specific variable or metric to display in tables. The basic use of the text feature is to highlight the same variable or metric with different aggregate values. The dropdown to the right of the word "Text" allows you to alter the alignment of the text.

Continuing from the last example, click Show Me!, choose Text Table (Crosstab) and OK. Note that the Label shelf has turned into the Text shelf.

The Label shelf changes to Text for text table views

Pages	Columns	Measure Names	
	Rows	Market	Product Type

Filters
- Market
- Measure Names

Market	Product Type	Avg. Profit	Profit
Central	Coffee	$61	$23,264
	Espresso	$82	$23,601
	Herbal Tea	$74	$24,757
	Tea	$66	$22,330
East	Coffee	$184	$30,992
	Espresso	$26	$6,244
	Herbal Tea	$30	$6,423
	Tea	$69	$15,668
West	Coffee	$28	$8,725
	Espresso	$66	$23,870
	Herbal Tea	$84	$26,303
	Tea	$42	$15,098

Marks

Automatic ▾

Text ▾ Measure Val..
Color ▾ ■
Size

Level of Detail

Measure Values
- AVG(Profit)
- SUM(Profit)

3. _Color_: this gives you the ability to highlight the view with a range or spectrum of colors for measure items or discrete colors for categorical dimension items. **Type <CTRL>-Z to undo the last step, returning to the bar chart. Add** _Market Size_ **to the Color shelf.** The default colors are assigned from the "Tableau 10" color palette, which is too dark to easily see the text on the bars. To correct this, **double-click on one of the colored squares in the color legend**. The Edit Colors dialog appears. **Click on the "Select Color Palette" dropdown in the upper right of the dialog to change the palette to "Tableau 10 Light", then click the Assign Palette button and OK.** The view shows _Profit_ for each _Market_ and _Product Type_ with _Market Size_ color-encoded.

Modifying the view by placing _Market Size_ on the Color shelf

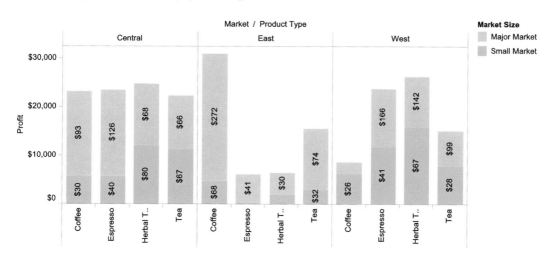

Next, click on the down carat next to Dimensions in the Data Items area and select Create Calculated Field from the menu. Name the field "Profit vs. Budget Profit". Enter the formula *Profit - Budget Profit* **by selecting the two separate measures from the Fields box and adding a minus sign between them. Move this new calculated item to the color shelf.** This will replace *Market Size*.

Creating and color encoding a new calculated field,
Profit vs. Budget Profit

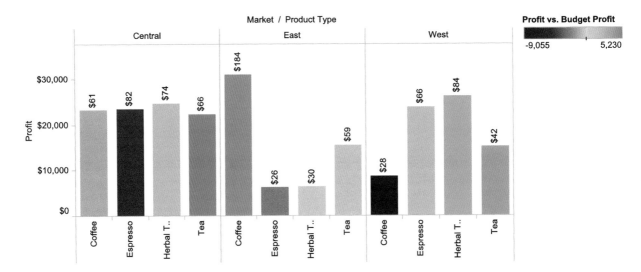

4. _Size_: allows you to alter the size of objects based on the range of values for the selected item. **Place** _Sales_ **on the Size shelf.** Note that the widths of the bars change, notably for Espresso, Herbal Tea and Tea in the East market. Size can be a useful means of conveying the relative impact of a related measure on the primary measure being examined. Notice that size is less precise to interpret than the bar heights, with the bar heights being much easier to distinguish differences among.

Modifying the view by placing _Sales_ on the Size shelf

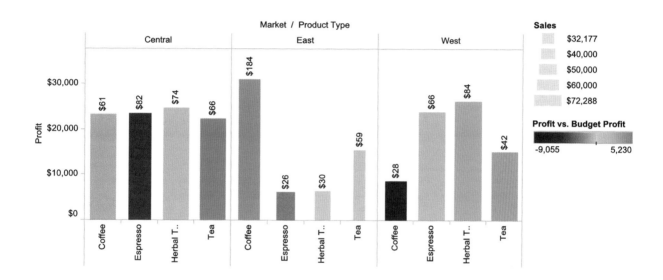

5. _Shape_: you can use this shelf to control the shapes that display the data from a categorical dimension item. **Click on Show Me! and select Scatter (Matrix)- graph.** This view type displays all measures in the matrix with *Product Type* color-encoded and *Market* shape-encoded.

This is an advanced view type that is fairly overwhelming for audiences that are infrequent consumers of data presented in graphs. This can be a good view type to quickly identify key trends and display those relationships in other, simpler chart types.

Modifying the view in two clicks using Show Me!

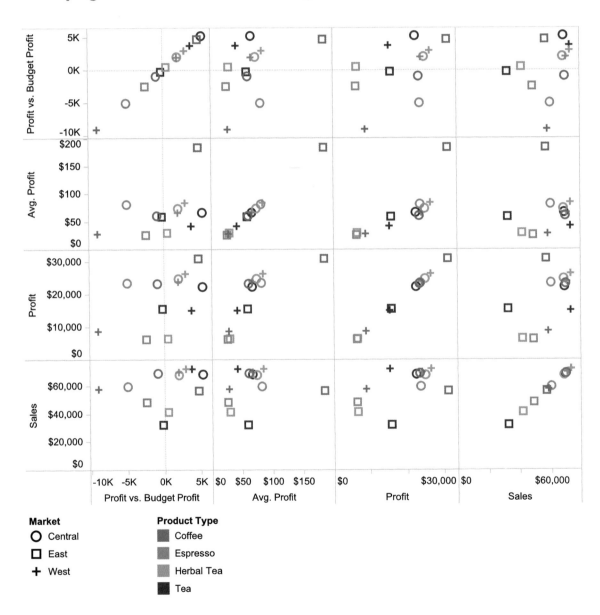

This is a fascinating view that allows the exploration of many questions. One step a product manager may take is to highlight all coffee products in the scatter matrix to explore how coffee is performing relative to tea for these metrics. **From the Color legend, hold down the <Ctrl> key and click on Coffee and then Espresso.** The selected items are now highlighted in the legend and the graph and all other items are grayed out, enabling easy comparison of coffee and espresso products against tea and herbal tea.

Highlighting Coffee and Espresso products only

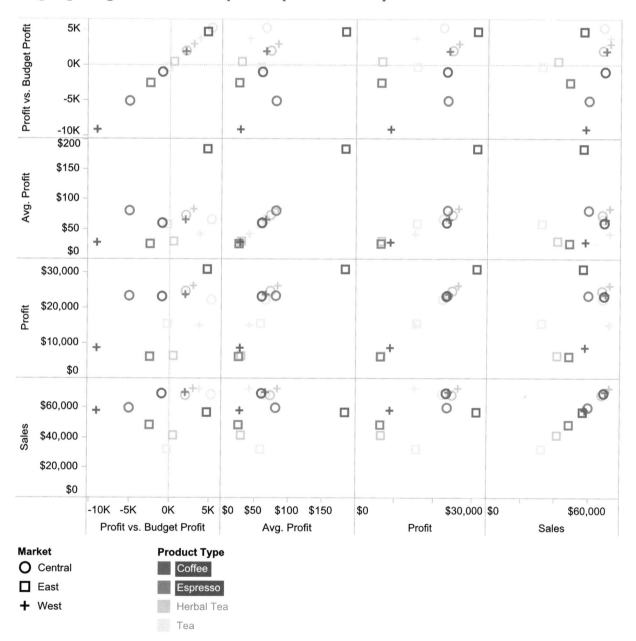

Market
- ◯ Central
- ☐ East
- ✚ West

Product Type
- ■ Coffee
- ■ Espresso
- ■ Herbal Tea
- ■ Tea

6. <u>*Level of Detail*</u>: the level of detail shelf controls the level at which data are summarized in your view. Using dimensional data items, the level of detail allows you to show more detail in your view without additional color or shape encoding. This is different from filtering, as it does not exclude data from the view, it simply divides and expands the data marks displayed in your view.

Remove all of the items from the Columns shelf except *Sum(Sales)* **and all items from the Rows shelf except** *Sum(Profit)*. **Note that you can use the <Ctrl> key to select multiple items on the shelves instead of dragging them one-by-one. Also, remove** *Market* **from the Shape shelf.** The graph will now have four data points. **Add** *Product* **to the Level of Detail shelf.** The data points show each product type (color-encoded) at the product level of detail, so there are now thirteen marks.

Modify the view by placing *Product* on the Level of Detail shelf

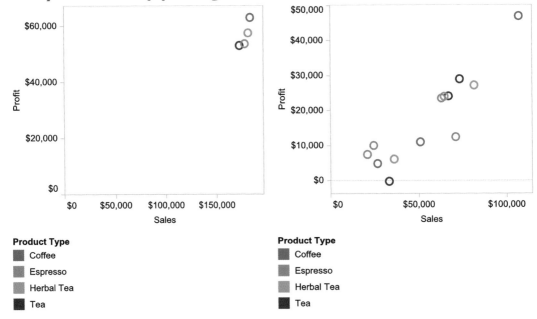

Place *Area Code* **on the Level of Detail shelf.**

Place *Area Code* on the Level of Detail shelf
to see more information (more rows returned and more marks shown)

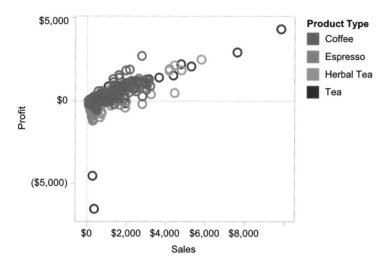

Finally, to show the greatest amount of detail, **use the main menu to turn off all aggregation via Analysis → Aggregate Measures**. Note that once you turn off this option, the Columns and Rows items along with the axis titles removed the aggregate functions from their names, since no aggregation is occurring! **All available data rows will be retrieved from your data source without aggregation, potentially returning an overwhelming amount of data.** Shrink the data points by moving the slider under the Size shelf to the left.**

Modify the view by turning off aggregation and resizing the points

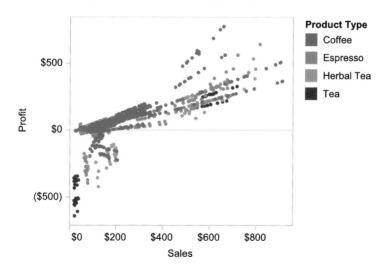

The Summary Card- rapid data insights

The Summary Card describes the measures currently shown in the view. Five summary statistics are listed- Count, Sum, Average, Minimum, and Maximum. If you have data items on the Pages and/or Filters shelves, the Summary Card will show only the data included in the current view. **Turn this on from the main menu by View → Summary.** To copy the summary card values to the clipboard, **click on the drop down arrow from the card and select Copy to Clipboard.**

Summary Card of all measures in a view

Summary	
Count:	3576
SUM(Profit)	
SUM:	$227,065
AVG:	$63
MIN:	($638)
MAX:	$778
SUM(Sales)	
SUM:	$715,885
AVG:	$200
MIN:	$17
MAX:	$912

If you would like to summarize certain data points in the view, such as the data in the upper right part of the graph, you can update the Summary Card by selecting the data within the view itself. **Hold the left mouse button down and drag your mouse pointer across the data point region that you want to highlight.** The Summary Card automatically updates the statistics based on the current selection.

Summary Card of measures for upper right part of graph,
note that only the bolded points in the graph are used in the summary

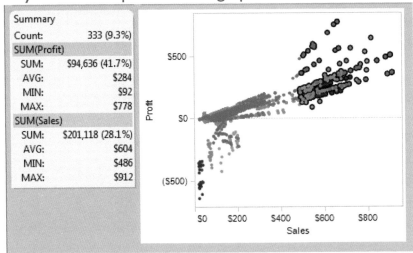

Headers and Axes

Headers and axes are automatically created by Tableau whenever items are placed on the Columns or Rows shelves. By default, a measure is represented by an axis with continuous values and a dimension is represented by a discrete or categorical header. **Please reset your view to the default layout found at the beginning of this chapter by selecting** *Market*, *Product Type* **and** *Profit*, **click Show Me!, and then click OK.** The figure shows *Profit* (a measure) as a continuous axis and *Market* and *Product Type* (dimensions) as headers.

Profit (measure) as a continuous axis and
Market and *Product Types* (dimensions) as headers

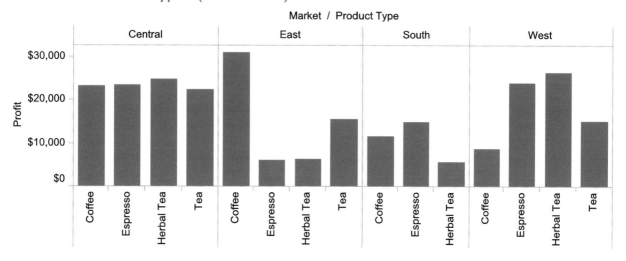

Tableau offers significant control over the layout of axis scales (formatting and appearance of the header and number fonts, orientation, etc. will be covered later in this chapter). **Right-click on the vertical or y-axis labeled** *Profit* **and select Edit Axis.** The Edit Axis dialog appears. Here you can change overall axis range, axis ranges across header groups in columns or rows, scale reversal or logarithmic scaling and tick mark formatting. You also can rename the axis by typing the new names in the title and subtitle fields. As shown in the figure below, **change the range by selecting Fixed and entering 0 in the Start field and 40,000 in the End field. Change the title to "2-Year Total Profits", and click OK to apply the changes and close the dialog**.

Edit Axis dialog box

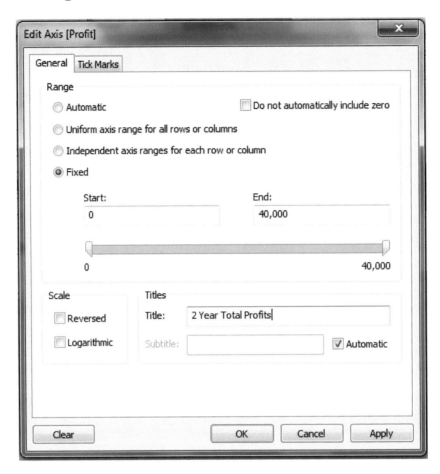

You can modify the headers in a similar manner. Right-click on a header value for *Product Type* (Espresso for example) and you will see four options related to the layout of the header: Format…, Rotate Label, Show Header and Edit Alias. Format allows control over the appearance of the header text and is covered later in this chapter. Rotate Label will rotate the header labels 90 degrees counterclockwise, changing the orientation of the text from horizontal to vertical or vice versa. Show Header controls whether or not the header text is displayed for the view. Edit Alias allows you to give particular values within categorical dimensions new labels to use as headers in the view.

Right-click on the "Herbal Tea" header and select Edit Alias… The Edit Alias dialog appears as shown in the figure below. **Change the Name for Herbal Tea to Decaf Tea, then click OK.** The view updates (shown below).

Renaming the alias of the Herbal Tea in the Edit Alias dialog box

Modified title on the vertical axis and
header alias in the horizontal axis

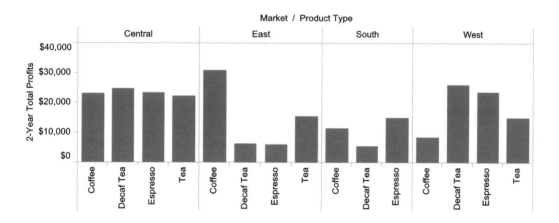

Titles, Captions, Field Labels and Legends

Titles enable quick identification of the content and purpose of your view. By default, the Title is the same as the worksheet name. **Modify the title by selecting View → Title on the main menu to bring up the title shelf, and then double-click on the current title to bring up the Edit Title dialog. Rename the sheet "Stephen".**

Captions typically present more detail about the contents of the view than the Title. Tableau automatically creates a caption based on the view layout, but you can manually modify it. **On the main menu, select View → Caption to place the Caption card in the view. Double-click on the caption or click on the down carat at the right of the Caption card to edit the caption.** In this case, do not change anything so that the default caption will be displayed.

Field labels are the dimension items used to create the headers and are automatically displayed with the headers. For example, in the previous figure in the Header and Axes section, the field label is "*Market / Product Type*". In this case, you can hide the field labels by **right-clicking on *Market / Product Type* and selecting Hide Field Label for Columns.**

When data values are encoded by color, shape and/or size, legends are the keys to understanding the encoding. In Tableau, each legend can be customized individually.

To follow the example, code the following data items: **On the Marks card, change the value in the dropdown from Automatic to Shape and put** *Market Size* **on both the Shape selector and the Color shelf. Place** *Marketing* **on the Size shelf. Simply click on the down carat on any individual Legend shelf and select Edit Colors, Sizes, etc. to customize the legends.**

Changing the title, automatic caption as view footnote,
hiding the field labels, and customizing size/shape/color legends

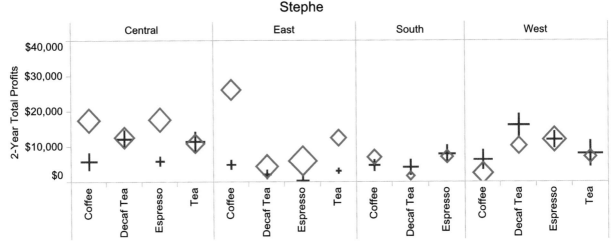

Sum of Profit for each Product Type broken down by Market. Color shows details about Market Size. Size shows sum of Marketing Shape shows details about Market Size

Marketing		**Market Size**		**Market Size**	
○	$592	◇ Major Market		▩ Major Market	
○	$2,000	+ Small Market		■ Small Market	
○	$4,000				
○	$6,000				
○	$8,000				
○	$10,000				
○	$11,278				

Formatting values in your Views

Tableau is extremely flexible and allows you to format all elements in the view. **Right-click on any element in the view and select Format.** The Format dialog appears in place of the Data Items window on the far left of the screen.

The Format dialog stays visible **until you close it by clicking on the x in the upper right corner of the dialog.** Within the Format dialog, the options vary based on your selected item. For example, in the figure below, the Format dialog on the left side is entitled "Format Product Type". **Click on one of the icons at the top of the format dialog or click on a different item in the view so another element of the view can be edited.** The right side of the figure is the "Format Shading" dialog.

Examples of Format dialog boxes

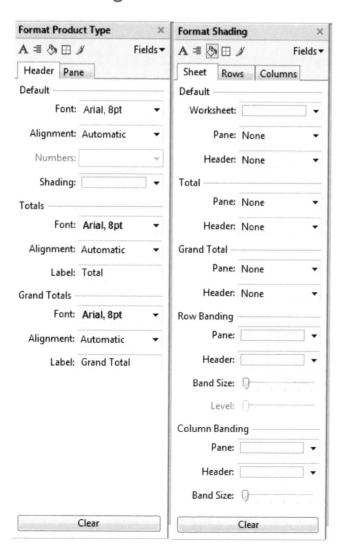

The symbols across the top of the Format dialog represent the various elements that can be formatted. From left to right, the symbols are Font, Alignment, Shading, Borders, and Lines, and on the far right is a dropdown menu for the Fields that you are currently using in your view. Formatting of Font, Alignment, Shading, Borders and Lines can be performed at the overall Sheet, Rows or Columns level. Marks can be formatted only at the overall Sheet level. Formatting can be copied from one sheet to another – even across workbooks.

It is easy to format the text of the headers and axes to reproduce the next figure. **Right-click on the vertical axis (2-Year Total Profits) and select Format.** The Format dialog appears. **In the Font field, select tan from the color palette.** This changes the font color. **Using the Fields dropdown menu, change the data item to** *Product Type*. **In the Font field, select tan from the color palette and select the italic box to italicize the text.**

Formatting text of headers and axes

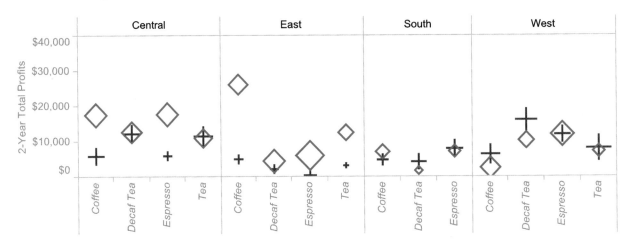

Chapter 7

Organizing the data in your Views- Sorting, Filtering, Aggregations, Percentages, Spotlighting, Totals/Subtotals, and Motion Charts

Chapter Highlights

- Sorting your views for clarity

- Filtering your views to find the right information

- Aggregating measures- sums, averages and more

- Use percentages to find the right ratios

- Spotlighting your view to call out key information

- Totals and subtotals

- Motion Charts and connecting to a new data source

This chapter will cover many of the features in Tableau that control how the data appear in your view once you have added the desired items to the shelves. This includes arranging your view, hiding irrelevant or confusing information, adjusting how measures are calculated, enabling the use of percentages to understand parts of the whole or ratios, spotlighting or calling out certain values, adding subtotals and totals to your view. At the end of the chapter, you will build a motion chart to follow the relationships between your data items over time, using new data. For the first time, you will be connecting to a new dataset that is not included with the software.

This chapter covers a lot of material in-depth, especially with all the new capabilities added in Tableau 6, so you might need more time than other chapters to be comfortable with this content.

For most of this chapter, you will use a sample data source provided by Tableau, the **Sample Coffee Chain** database. **For the motion chart, you need to download and save a new dataset from the Freakalytics website, the *Winery customers and sales* dataset.** It is available at http://www.Freakalytics.com/rgts6

Simple and advanced sorting of views

Tableau automatically sorts your data along dimensional items used in your view. By default, it sorts the category labels in ascending alphabetical order. For example, Tea, Coffee and Espresso are sorted as Coffee, Espresso and Tea.

It may be useful to sort your view by the measure in use. The quickest way to sort by the measure is **to click on the Sort ascending or Sort descending buttons on the Tableau toolbar**, shown in the figure below.

Sort ascending and Sort descending buttons on the toolbar

For example, you may want to sort your market regions so that they are ordered in the view from highest to lowest profit. **In the Coffee Chain dataset, select** *Market, Product Type* **and** *Profit*, **and click Show Me! and OK.** To obtain the unsorted view on the left in the figure, **remove** *Product Type* **from the Columns shelf.** To see the view on the right, **click on the Sort descending button.** The Sort buttons are quite powerful, as they use the inputs from your selection to infer the type of sort that you want.

Aligned bar views with *Profit* by *Market*: left view-unsorted, right view-sorted via the Sort descending toolbar button

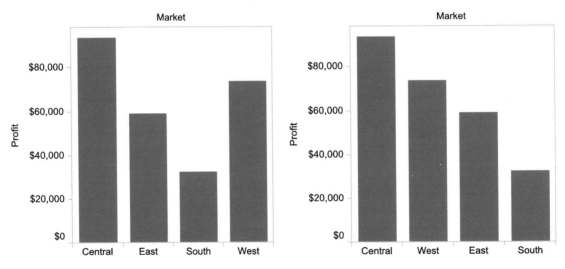

A variety of advanced sorting methods is available beyond the default alphabetic item sorting by dimension and the sort ascending and descending toolbar items by measure. **Right-click on** *Market* **on the Columns shelf and select Sort.** The Sort dialog box will appear as shown in the next figure, which can be used with dimensional items on the Columns or Rows shelf.

Sort dialog box

! *Alternate Route:* You also can directly drag and reorder items in legends or rows and columns to manually sort them.

From the Sort dialog, you can sort data by the order of the original data source, alphabetically, by any field in your data source, or manually for custom sorting. At the top of the dialog, you can specify either Ascending or Descending order, applicable for alphabetic and field sort options. **In this example, select Sort by Field →** *Sales***, then Descending order, and click OK** to yield the figure below. Note that the Sort order field is grayed out until you select a field. This sort results in a different order than descending profit, which is surprising since you would typically expect a strong relationship between sales and profit.

Using the Sort dialog box to Sort by Field

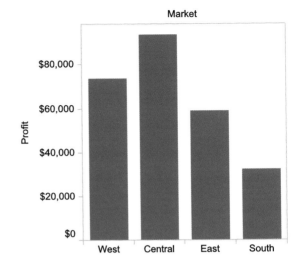

Although you will need to keep *Sales* sorted for the next example, in general all sorting can be cleared by **right-clicking on the dimension item in the Columns or Rows shelf and selecting Clear Sort.**

! *Performance Tip*: The major difference between the one-click Sort buttons and the Sort dialog is that one-click is 'one time' and does not automatically update as the dataset or view updates. Specifying the sort from the dialog with Descending or Ascending Sort Order activated re-sorts every time the view is updated.

Simple and advanced filtering of views

Filters reduce the data that are displayed in your view by allowing you to select a subset of the data. Filters can be specified using dimension or measure items, although the two types have different dialogs and options.

The simplest filter uses the labels of dimension items or marks in the view. **To filter by dimension item, right-click on a label or multiple labels in the view, or the data marks themselves, selecting either Keep Only or Exclude.** Both options will create a filter on the dimension item, keeping or excluding the selected items.

To create the next example, **continue from the last example by placing** *State* **on the Color shelf and** *Profit* **on the Label shelf.** Filtering of dimension items is also available by dragging the item from the Dimensions pane to the Filters shelf. For example, **drag** *State* **from the Dimensions pane to the Filters shelf.** The Filter dialog appears, as shown in the figure below. There are four tabs available: General, Wildcard, Condition, and Top. The General tab (displayed in the figure) allows selection of the filter criteria by label. **Click None and then select California, Florida and Illinois, and then click OK.**

Filter dialog box with General tab displayed and resulting view

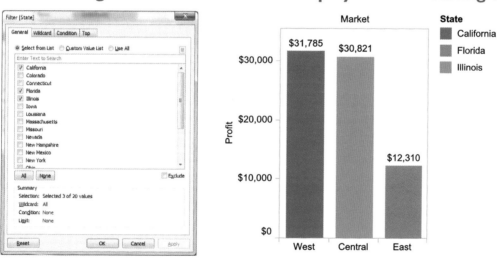

The Condition tab allows filtering the view using any data field with an aggregate function condition such as Sum, Average and Count (aggregations will be discussed in detail later in the chapter). Before switching to the Condition tab, **open the** *State* **filter by double-clicking it on the Filters shelf, and then choose Use All on the General tab. From the Condition tab, choose By Field → ** *Sales* **→ Sum → greater than (>), enter 60,000 and click OK.** This is shown in the next figure.

Filter dialog box with Condition tab displayed and resulting view

To continue with this example, **bring up the *State* filter again by clicking on the down carat on *State* on the Filters shelf. Click None on the Condition tab, then click on the Top tab**. The Top tab allows you to filter the view using the top or bottom rankings of any data field with an aggregate function condition, such as the ten states with the lowest sales. **Choose By Field → Bottom →10 → *Sales* → Sum and click OK.** This is shown in the next figure with only the Bottom 10 States showing.

Filter dialog box with Top tab displayed and resulting view

! *Performance Tip:* A dimension filter is applied independently of all the other filters, so the condition and top elements will not consider other filters in play unless you add those other filters to the Context. A Context Filter is a special type of filter that forces the creation of a temporary database table before proceeding with other filters.

108

Aggregations for measures- specify the right summaries

Tableau automatically assigns an aggregate function to all items that are measures. By default, the aggregate function for non-geographic measures is to *Sum* the data. Each cell or value used to create the view is included when Tableau calculates aggregates. Other common aggregations include *Average* and *Count*. Average is similar to the mean of all the records in a cell and Count is the number of records available in the data source for the cell. Less commonly used aggregations include *Minimum, Maximum, Standard Deviation, Standard Deviation (Population), Variance,* and *Variance (Population)*.

When you use Tableau Data Extracts instead of other local data sources such as Excel or CSV files, two additional aggregates are available: *Median* and *Count Distinct*. The Median is literally the "middle" data value. If you sort all of the values for a data item from lowest to highest, the Median is the value in the middle of this list. The Median is useful if your data has a few extreme values that may skew the Mean value. For example, you may have sales amounts of $100, $200, $300, $400 and $5,000. The Mean of these numbers is $1,200, but the Median is $300. Notice that the Mean is not close to any actual data value, while the Median is a typical outcome.

Count Distinct is useful for counting the unique names of a data item in your data source. For example, suppose Joe placed 3 orders, Katy placed 8 orders and Patty placed 22 orders. The Count of the data item *First Name* would be 33, but the Count Distinct would be 3, since there are only 3 distinct names in the data item.

In general, you can change the default aggregation from the measures part of the Data shelf **by right-clicking on the item and selecting Field Properties → Aggregation.** Once a measure item is added to the view, you can also customize the aggregation for the current view. **On the shelf where the item is placed, click on the down carat in the oval of the measure item. Select Measure and pick the desired aggregation function.**

Now you will develop an intricate view of three aggregations for the same data item, *Profit*. **Create a new worksheet using the Coffee Chain data source. Duplicate** *Profit* **three times by right-clicking on in the Measures pane and selecting Duplicate. Change the aggregate of the first copy to Average (AVG) by right-clicking on it, selecting Field Properties → Aggregation → Average, and naming it** *Avg. Profit*. **Change the second copy to Maximum (MAX) and name it** *Max. Profit*. **Change the third copy to Minimum (MIN) and name it** *Min. Profit*.

Place *Market* **and** *Product Type* **on the Columns shelf. Change Mark type from Automatic to Shape. Add Measure Names to the Shape and Color shelves. If the warning pops up, accept "Add all members"** (this is fine here, but with very large data sources in the real world, this could take a long time). **Add Measure Values to the Label and Rows shelves.** You will see that Measure Names is automatically on the Filters shelf.

Double-click on it and select None, turn on *Avg. Profit*, *Max. Profit* **and** *Min. Profit* **and click OK.**

Change the Colors for *Max. Profit* **to Green,** *Min. Profit* **to Red and** *Avg. Profit* **to Blue. Change the Shapes for** *Max. Profit* **to a down triangle,** *Min. Profit* **to an up triangle, and** *Avg. Profit* **to a filled-in circle. Format the Measure Values axis to be currency with no decimal places.**

Applying three aggregations to the same measure item, *Profit*

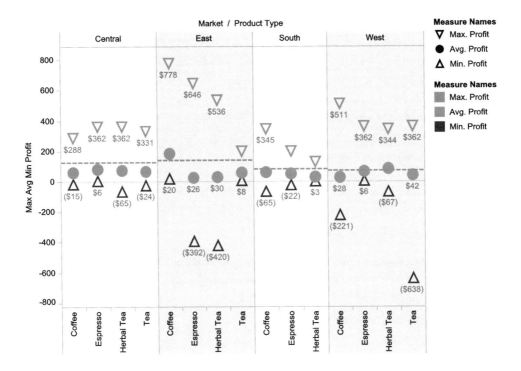

By applying multiple aggregations to the same measure, you can gain additional insights compared to having only a single aggregation view.

Percentages provide balance to compare ratios

Using percentages in Tableau is easy and informative. Percentages allow the rapid comparison of cells across columns and/or rows when the total amounts vary widely across cells. Percentages can be calculated as a percentage of all values, a percentage of values in a row or column, and a percentage of values in a cell. Other less common percentage calculations are also available.

For the next example, in the Coffee Chain dataset, select *Market*, *Product Type* **and** *Profit*, **and click Show Me! and OK. Add** *Market* **to the Color shelf and** *Market Size* **to the beginning of the Rows shelf before** *SUM (Profit)*. The profit for each product type in each region and market size is shown in the first view.

Perhaps you are more interested in understanding the relative contribution of each product type to a region/market size. Since various panes where *Region* and *Market Size* intersect have different total profit, it is hard to gauge the relative contribution of each product type to a pane. To simplify this comparison, **from the main menu select Analysis → Percentage of → Pane.** This will change the metric calculation from *Profit* to *Percentage of Total Profit* for a pane, as shown below.

Profit (left) and Percentage of Total Profit (right)
for each Product Type, by Region and Market Size

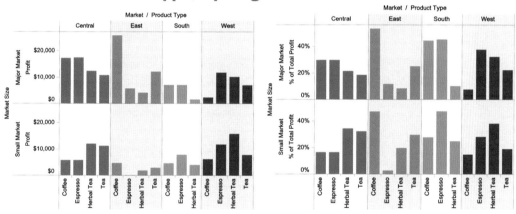

In the original view, overall profits in the South were much lower than the other regions. Once the view was adjusted to show the percentage of profit within each pane, the bars were adjusted based on the total profit in each pane, with each pane totaling 100%. This is very useful if you want to highlight the relative contribution to profit of each product in a particular market.

Spotlighting your View to call out important values

Spotlighting is a powerful feature in Tableau used to highlight measure values in a table or chart that meet criteria defined by you, typically by color encoding. For example, you may want to highlight products that have profits above $10,000 or below $3,000 to emphasize that they require additional discussion and research. Using spotlighting, you can make these products "jump" off the page.

To follow this example, **in Coffee Chain, select** *Market*, *Product Type* **and** *Profit*, **and click Show Me! and OK. Then, move** *Market* **from the Columns shelf to the Rows shelf and add** *Product* **to the end of the Columns shelf. From the Data Items / Measures pane, right-click on** *Profit* **and select Create Calculated Field.** The Calculated Field dialog appears. **Change the name of the Calculated Field to "Profit Spotlight" and enter the Formula as:**

IF SUM([Profit]) >= 10000 THEN "Best"
ELSEIF SUM([Profit]) <= 3000 THEN "Worst" (Note that the "ELSEIF" function is one word.)
ELSE "Middle of the Pack" END

The dialog should confirm it is a valid calculation, but if an error message pops up, check your formula for typos. **Click OK.** *Profit Spotlight*, the calculated item, will appear in the Data Items / Measures pane. **Double-click on the item and it is automatically added to the Color selector of the Marks shelf.**

A color legend card appears. **Double-click on the Best color.** The Edit Colors dialog appears. **Change Best to green, Middle of the Pack to gray, and Worst to red, and then click OK. Right-click on South and West in the view and select Exclude.** Only Central and East will be displayed in the view.

Spotlighting *Products* with the Best and Worst *Profits* by color encoding (only Central and East markets shown)

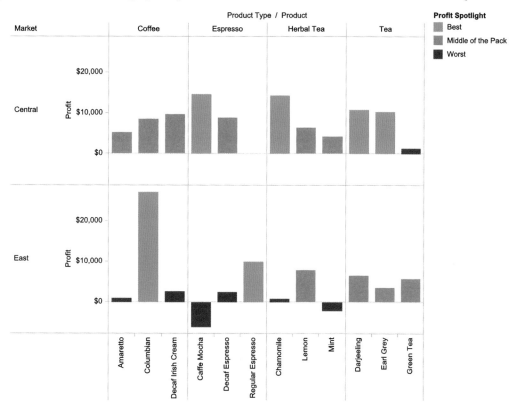

In this case, spotlighting makes it easy to see that Central has only one underperforming product, the products with the highest profits are different between Central and East, and East has many more underperforming products but also has the highest profit product.

! *Alternate Route:* This is a simple example that also can be done by using the Stepped Color function on the Edit Colors dialog. Editing the default color range can give the same effect with less effort than the calculation. Note that this alternate approach has less control over the exact cutoffs for color coding, so it is not always a better choice.

! *Performance Tip:* The advantage of using Spotlighting over the Create Calculated Field function is that values of interest that do not appear in your current dataset may appear in future datasets. These will be spotlighted automatically in the manner that you specify.

Totals and Subtotals to sum up parts of your view

Totals and Subtotals give you the powerful ability to summarize your view at the view pane level (the crossing of categorical item values used in the view) or as a grand total or totals for rows and/or columns. Due to the nature of subtotals, they are available only if there are at least two dimensional items in either the Rows or Columns shelf.

Although the function includes the word "total", Tableau does not simply add up all the values - it uses the aggregation specified for the measures in your view. Therefore, totals for summed measures would be the sum of the sums in each cell, but the total for averaged measures would be the average of the underlying data values used in the cells.

Some words of caution: *if you are using a pre-summarized data source for your view and an aggregate function other than Count or Sum, Tableau could return wrong values for subtotals or grand totals.* Tableau calculates the totals based on the original data, it does not calculate the total based on the results displayed. *Also be careful to not sum percentages- these should be averaged!*

Now, you are going to build upon the example from the previous section on spotlighting. **Duplicate the sheet, click on Show Me! and change the view type to Text Table (Cross-tab).** Exclude the Coffee and Tea product types from the view, **by clicking on Coffee, <Ctrl> and then Tea, then right-click and select Exclude. Add** *Market Size* **to the end of the Rows shelf. In the main menu, click on Table → Add All Subtotals.**

Adding Subtotals to a spotlighted Text Table

| | | Product Type / Product | | | | | | | |
| | | Espresso | | | | Herbal Tea | | | |
Market	Market Size	Caffe Mocha	Decaf Espresso	Regular Espresso	Total	Chamo..	Lemon	Mint	Total
Central	Major Market	$11,457	$6,154		$17,611	$6,439	$2,083	$4,069	$12,591
	Small Market	$3,185	$2,705		$5,890	$7,996	$4,170		$12,166
	Total	$14,642	$8,859		$23,501	$14,435	$6,253	$4,069	$24,757
East	Major Market	($6,069)	$1,738	$10,274	$5,943	$764	$6,955	($3,369)	$4,350
	Small Market	($163)	$673	($209)	$301		$947	$1,126	$2,073
	Total	($6,232)	$2,411	$10,065	$6,244	$764	$7,902	($2,243)	$6,423

Profit Spotlight
- Best
- Middle of the Pack
- Worst

Note that profits from all products and market sizes have been summed in the table. However, grand totals are not shown, which would summarize across all markets or across all product types. Turn off Subtotals by **choosing Table → Remove All Subtotals on the main menu.** Turn on Grand Totals for both Rows and Columns: **Select Table → Row Grand Totals and Table → Column Grand Totals.**

Adding Grand Totals to a spotlighted Text Table

| | | Product Type / Product | | | | | | | |
| | | Espresso | | | Herbal Tea | | | Grand Total |
Market	Market Size	Caffe Mocha	Decaf Espresso	Regular Espresso	Chamo..	Lemon	Mint	
Central	Major Market	$11,457	$6,154		$6,439	$2,083	$4,069	$30,202
	Small Market	$3,185	$2,705		$7,996	$4,170		$18,056
East	Major Market	($6,069)	$1,738	$10,274	$764	$6,955	($3,369)	$10,293
	Small Market	($163)	$673	($209)		$947	$1,126	$2,374
Grand Total		$8,410	$11,270	$10,065	$15,199	$14,155	$1,826	$60,925

Profit Spotlight
- Best
- Middle of the Pack
- Worst

In general, subtotals and grand totals are less useful when using bar or line chart views. Often, the totals greatly surpass the individual values, resetting the values on the axis labels and making the chart difficult to read. Totals are often more useful and easier to include on histograms, pie charts, and maps, or aggregations other than Sum and Count, such as Average, Minimum and Maximum.

Motion Charts with Advanced Page Filter Feature

Motion charts were popularized by Hans Rosling, an eminent statistician and doctor specializing in public health, during a presentation he gave at a TED conference, a global organization that focuses on innovative ideas. He discussed the lifespans and health of people across many countries and how that has changed over time with societal and medical care advancements. A motion chart is great for this type of dataset- it is a simple yet powerful display that shows how the relationship of two measures (e.g., sales and profitability) changes over time. Usually, a category is divided into its members (e.g., the product line category is split into coffee, espresso, and tea).

Using marketing data for a boutique winery, you will create a standard motion chart in Tableau, which is a scatter plot combined with features of the Pages Filter shelf. Note that the concept is also applicable to other chart types. In this case, the marketing manager of the winery is asking: "How does the relationship between customer segment and preferred marketing channel vary over time?"

If you've haven't already, **download and save the *Winery sales and customers* data from the Freakalytics web site at** <u>**http://www.Freakalytics.com/rgts6**</u> Once downloaded, you'll connect to a new local data source.

On the main menu, **click Data → Connect to Data**, and the Connect to Data dialog appears. **Click Microsoft Excel and Next.** The Excel Workbook Connection dialog appears. **Click the Browse button, navigate to the location of the Excel workbook, and select it.** The worksheet names appear in *Step 2: Select the worksheet (table) area to analyze.* **Select Sales data. Keep the default values for Steps 3 and 4 and click OK.**

Connect to Data and Excel Workbook Connection dialogs

 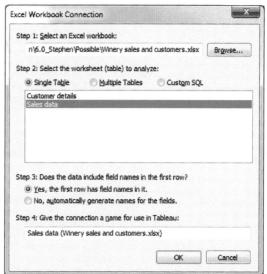

The Data Connection dialog appears with three choices: *Connect live* (connects directly to your data, *Import all data* (imports entire data source as a Tableau Data Extract) or *Import some data* (imports a subset of your data as a Tableau Data Extract).

The Data Connection dialog

Select the first choice- *Connect live*. You are now connected to your data! **Then you can save this work as a predefined data connection on the main menu: Data → Data Connection → Export.**

For simplicity, the method to build a motion chart is broken down into four steps.

Step 1. **Open the Winery customer and sales dataset. Select** *Customer Segment,* *Email Sales* **and** *Tasting Room Sales.* **Click Show Me! and accept the default chart type, Scatter (Single) by clicking OK.** **Change the aggregate for both metrics in the view from SUM to AVG. Additionally, format both data items as Currency.**

Step 1. The foundation for the motion chart.

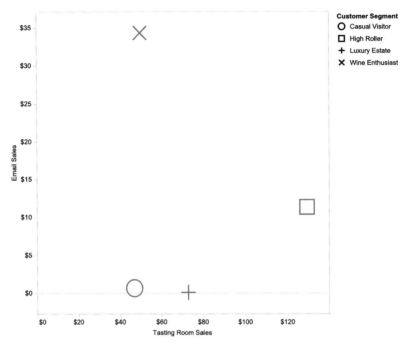

Step 2. **Move** *Customer Segment* **from the Shape shelf to the Label shelf. Change the mark type from Automatic to Text. The Label shelf turns into the Text shelf. On the Text shelf, <CTRL>-click and hold on** *Customer Segment*, **then drag it to the Color shelf** (this creates a copy of the item so you can place it on another shelf).

! *Performance Tip:* If you have about 6-8 data points or less, you may want to label the data points with their names spelled out in text to make the final motion chart easier to follow.

Step 2. Prior to setting the chart in motion

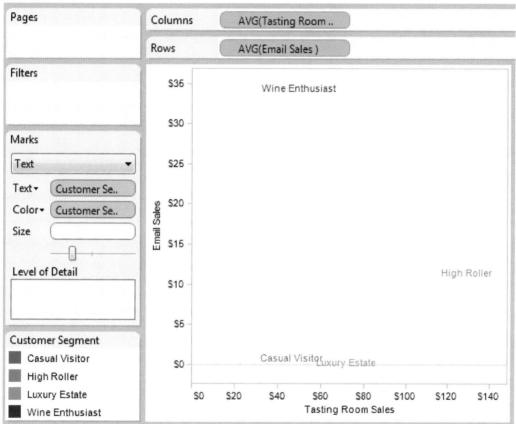

The Wine Enthusiast group responds very strongly to Email marketing, as the average spend is much higher than the other groups, but the High Rollers spend more during Tasting Room visits. Although this is useful information, now the marketing manager is curious about how this relationship has changed over time. This is where the motion chart becomes priceless (and perhaps entertaining)!

Step 3. **Add** *Date* **to the Pages shelf twice.** It will automatically switch to the *Year* and *Quarter* level of detail and now appears in the Pages Filter Control with an initial value of **2008, Q3**.

Step 3. Initial motion chart view

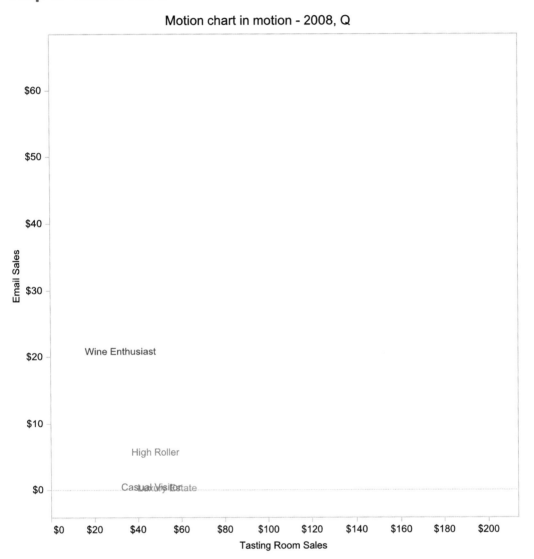

Unlike the Filters shelf, when you place items on the Pages shelf, Tableau incorporates the full range of values for each item in the Pages dropdown. Using the range of possible outcomes, Tableau scales the axes of your plot accordingly. Notice that the range of values is quite different from the earlier view, and that the values are much lower for the segments that were leading earlier.

Step 4. **On the Pages control panel, click the checkbox for *Show History*.** Nothing changes as you page through the graph. However, if you first click on one of the segments in the graph, the default history behavior turns on. It may be helpful to make this feature stand out more. **On the Pages control panel, turn on the *Trail* option by clicking the drop-down chevron next to *Show History* and selecting Trails. Page through the views, and then click on a segment to bring up the trails.** The example shows the trails over 8 quarters for the top 2 segments. Note that you can select the desired segment at any point and the trails will track the previous history, so you do not have to select it before placing it on the shelf.

Step 4. Example of motion chart with trails for selected items

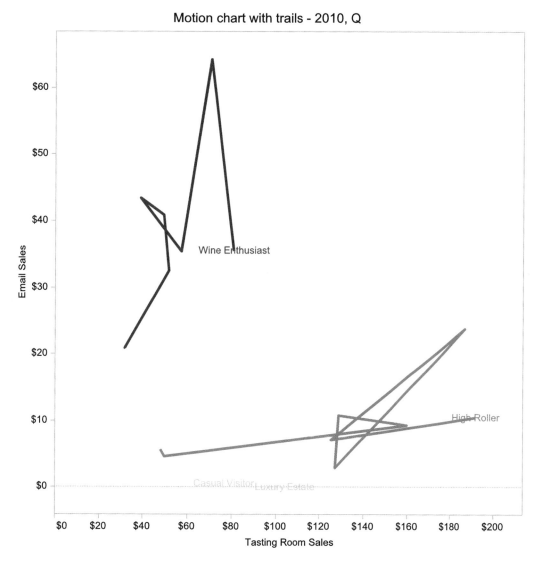

Motion chart with trails - 2010, Q

! *Performance Tip*: There is a wide array of additional options available with the ***Show History*** feature. Try them out!

The motion chart makes it easy to see the long-term direction of these two customer segments. For the High Rollers, the typical quarterly tasting room sales amount moved up considerably, growing by nearly 400% in two years. E-mail sales remained relatively flat, at around 100% growth. The marketing manager may be particularly interested to see that e-mail sales spiked in Q4 of 2009 (up 400% from baseline, but only in a single quarter), yet rapidly returned to their earlier growth trajectory. It is probably a good idea for him to review e-mails from that quarter to figure out the messaging that works with this segment.

Meanwhile, the Wine Enthusiast segment has grown in both tasting room and e-mail sales over the past two years, with a possibly important drop in e-mail sales for the current quarter versus their earlier trajectory. Overall, Wine Enthusiasts are up about 60% to 300% in e-mail sales (depending on whether the last quarter was just an anomaly or the direction of future sales) and a solid 150% in tasting room sales.

Chapter 8

Essential Calculations and Models- Quick Calculations, Custom Table Calculations, Reference Lines and Trend Lines

---

Chapter Highlights

- Quick table calculations- complex calculations made easy

- Custom table calculations- the power to calculate specific metrics

- Reference lines, bands and distributions to emphasize useful values

- Use Trend Lines to model your data

Now that you have experience in creating views, altering their appearance, and organizing them in useful ways, you are ready to move on to more complex manipulations of your view. This chapter will help you to answer advanced questions relatively quickly by optimizing the information displayed in your views. You will walk through several examples of quick calculations where most of the work is done for you, custom table calculations new to Tableau 6 which give you a lot of power to write complicated formulas, adding reference lines for quick review of your data, and development of trend lines that summarize overall data patterns, including some basic information about their interpretations and limitations. The goal is to give you an idea of the capabilities of Tableau, so that you are able to use them as a starting place for problems unique to your business.

You will be using two datasets: **Sample Coffee Chain** provided by Tableau and *Winery customers and sales,* which you may have downloaded and used in the last chapter. If not, **download and save it from the Freakalytics website at** http://www.Freakalytics.com/rgts6 .

Quick Table Calculations

Quick Table Calculations are often related to date views and are applied to measures used in the view. Quick Table Calculations include Running Total, Difference (versus prior period or cell), Percent Difference (versus prior period or cell), Percent of Total, Moving Average (smooth's out data that varies widely by time period), Year-to-Date Total (called YTD Total in Tableau), Compound Growth Rate, Year-over-Year Growth rate, Year-to-Date Growth (called YTD Growth in Tableau, and defined as cumulative YTD growth in measure over prior year.)

The example shown can be created by **selecting** *Date* **and** *Profit* **from the Coffee Chain dataset. Click Show Me! and select the default selection- Line (Discrete). Drill-down on the** *Date* **variable twice, from** *Year* **to** *Quarter* **and from** *Quarter* **to** *Month.* **This can be done by clicking on the plus sign next to the** *Date* **item on the Columns shelf.**

Add *Profit* **a second time to the Rows shelf. Then add** *Sales* **to the Rows shelf. For the second** *Profit* **item on the Rows shelf, click on the down carat and select Quick Table Calculation → YTD Total. For** *Sales* **on the Rows shelf, click on the down carat and select Quick Table Calculation → YTD Total. Drag the** *Year(Date)* **item from the Columns shelf to the Color selector on the Marks shelf.**

Quick Table Calculations- YTD Totals for *Profit* and *Sales* with *Year* in color

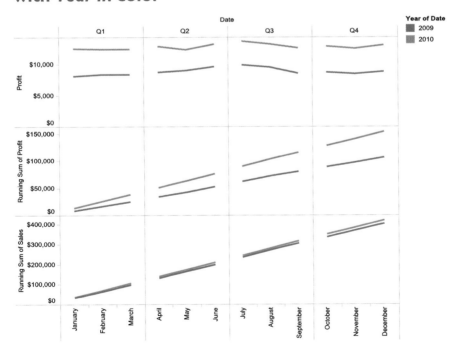

The Running Sums of *Profit* and *Sales* contrast quite dramatically. You can immediately observe very little difference in 2009 and 2010 sales growth through the year but substantially greater profit growth in 2010 over 2009. YTD running totals can help with estimating final sales and profit figures based on prior year patterns and current year trajectory. **Please save this worksheet as Quick Table, because you will come back to it for the next two examples.**

Custom Table Calculations using data in your views

Quick Table Calculations are fast, convenient and very helpful. However, if you are used to writing complex formulas in Excel, they may not get the whole job done. For people like you, Tableau 6 now gives you the power to go well beyond default table calculations!

As you saw in the last example, table calculations allow easy comparison between the year-to-date sales and year-to-date profit. **For this example, duplicate the sheet from the last section, Edit → Duplicate Sheet. Then delete all the measures except for Running Sum of Profit, which is the second** *SUM(Profit)* **on the Rows shelf.**

You can perform secondary table calculations on two types of table calculations: *running totals* and *moving calculations* (e.g., YTD Totals and Moving Averages.) One common secondary calculation is to determine the percent difference from the prior year for running totals. For example, if the YTD was $75,787 in June 2010, and the YTD was $51,963 in June 2009, the YTD % growth was 45.8%. To add this to the example as a label above the lines, **<CTRL>-click and hold on the** *SUM(Profit)* **data item on the Rows shelf and drag it to the Label shelf**. This will duplicate the item so it is now on the Rows and Label shelves. You will now see the YTD running total values on both lines.

On the Label shelf, click the drop-down caret and select Edit Table Calculation. The Table Calculation dialog appears. **Check** *Perform a secondary calculation on the result* **and the dialog will expand, change the** *Secondary Type* **to "Percent Difference From", change** *Calculate the difference along* **to "Date" and** *At the level* **to "Year of Date".** The dialog should appear like the example below. **Click OK.**

The Table Calculation dialog with secondary calculation

Secondary calculation determining the
percent difference from the prior year for running totals

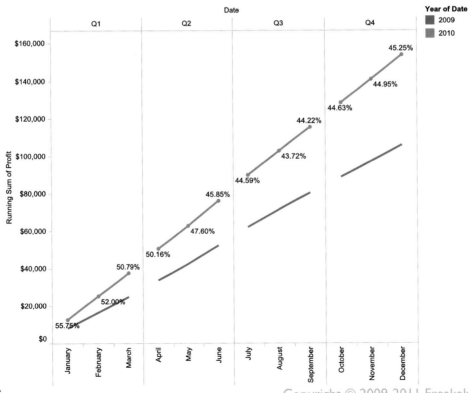

Here is a more advanced example that is very exciting to do in Tableau 6. In the past, if you wanted to view the running ratio of YTD profit over YTD sales (the YTD gross profit margin) you would have needed to return to Excel, write custom SQL or use another tool to calculate this value. Now, with full access to table calculations from the Calculated Field dialog, you can create complex calculations.

**For this example, duplicate the sheet from the Quick Table section, Edit →
Duplicate Sheet. For** *SUM(Sales)* **on the Rows shelf, click on the down carat and
select Edit Table Calculation.** The Table Calculation dialog appears. **Click the
Customize button and the Calculated Field dialog will appear.** It shows the formula
used by Tableau to show YTD sales, RUNNING_SUM(SUM([Sales])).

Complex table calculations using the calculated field dialog

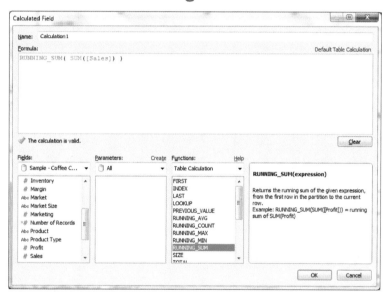

**! *Performance Tip*: If you click the Functions drop-down and change it from All
to Table Calculations, you will see all of the available functions.** With a bit of
imagination and practice, there is a huge array of possibilities once you understand these
functions!

To calculate YTD gross profit margin, enter this formula:
RUNNING_SUM(SUM([Profit])) / RUNNING_SUM(SUM([Sales]))
and change the Name to YTD Gross Margin. Click OK twice. YTD Gross Margin now
appears in the third row of the view.

Complex table calculations:
Profit, **YTD** *Profit* and **YTD** *Gross Margin*

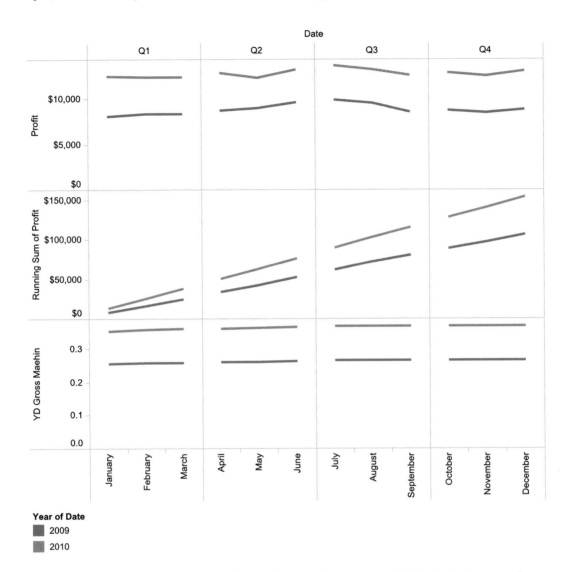

Year of Date
- 2009
- 2010

Now you are ready for an extremely advanced example of custom Table Calculations. **Open a new worksheet.** The next figure shows the average sales amount by state within each product at the Coffee Chain. The custom Table Calculation is used to show the percent difference in average sales for each state relative to the average state in each product. This value, *% above/below average order amount*, is used on the Color shelf and on the Label shelf. **You can create this field on the main menu, Analysis → Create Calculated Field, and enter:**

```
( AVG([Sales]) - WINDOW_AVG( AVG([Sales]) ) )
/
WINDOW_AVG( AVG([Sales]) )
```

! *Performance Tip*: Try to use the Fields and Functions selectors as much as possible to avoid typos in your formulas.

Place *Product* **on the Columns shelf. Place** *Sales* **on the Rows shelf, and change to average. Place** *% above/below average order amount* **on the Color shelf and the Label shelf. On the Label dropdown, keep *Show mark labels* checked, and under Marks to Label, select Min/Max so labels will be shown only for the states with minimum and maximum values, and choose Cell for the Scope. On the Marks Card, change Automatic to Shape, and then add** *State* **to the Shape shelf.** (If the warning appears, accept it by selecting "Add all members"). **Using Edit Shape, assign the open circle to every state except for Iowa, and then assign a filled-in diamond to Iowa. Turn on highlighting by state and select Iowa from the Shape legend. Sort by** *Product***, choosing Descending,** *Field* **Sales and then** *Aggregation* **Average.** This will give you the basic view- the one below has a couple more clean-up steps.

Average Sales Amount by State within each Product of the Coffee Chain, with percent above/below average order amount on Label and Color shelves

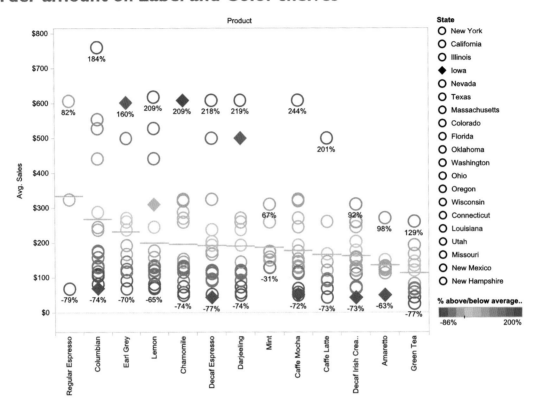

It is very interesting to see that Iowa has extreme product order variability. It is the top state in 2 of the 9 products sold there, yet it is also the bottom state for 5 of the 9 products sold there. This would definitely be an interesting topic for product or regional managers to investigate.

If you create this view and see different values, you should verify that Tableau is calculating the *% above/below average order amount* using *State*. This is the NOT the default behavior for table calculations, which is to use Table (Across) as the direction of computation. **To correct this, use the dropdown menus on the Label and Color shelves.**

Dropdown menu on the Color shelf to change default direction of computation

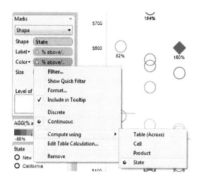

One final example of the power of custom table calculations to enhance your views is using the INDEX function. This returns the "row" number of an item based on the sorting used in your view. This example reinforces the importance of using the right sort order and Compute using item.

If you have not already used the Winery dataset, **download and save the *Winery sales and customers* data from the Freakalytics web site at** http://www.Freakalytics.com/rgts6 .

On the main menu, **click Data → Connect to Data**, and the Connect to Data dialog appears. **Click Microsoft Excel and Next.** The Excel Workbook Connection dialog appears. **Click the Browse button, navigate to the location of the Excel workbook, and select it.** The worksheet names appear in *Step 2: Select the worksheet (table) area to analyze.* **Select Sales data. Keep the default values for Steps 3 and 4 and click OK.**

The Data Connection dialog appears with three choices: **Select the first choice- *Connect live.*** You are now connected to your data! **Then you can save this work as a predefined data connection on the main menu: Data → Data Connection → Export.**

Now you are going to create a map of total newsletter sales (SUM) by state. *State* is not assigned the correct geographic role, **so right-click on** *State* **→ Geographic Role → State (Abbreviation). Double-click** *State* **and then double-click** *Sale Amount.* To zoom in on the map, **highlight the data points in the continental U.S., right-click on a data point and select Keep Only. Next, use the main menu, Analysis → Create Calculated Field, to create a new calculated field named RANK with the very simple Formula: INDEX( ) . Place the new item RANK on the Label shelf.** You will notice that all states appear to be ranked as "1", but clearly, this is incorrect.

Click the drop down on the RANK item from the Label shelf and change the *Compute using* value from Table (Across) to *State (Abbr).* Now, each state shows a unique value for rank, but it appears that the ranking is not by *Newsletter Sales* but rather by the alphabetic order of the state names (e.g., Washington is 47 even though it is the top state for *Newsletter Sales*.) To fix this last issue, **click the drop-down for the item** *State* **on the Level of Detail shelf, select Sort and set the sort to be Descending by** *Field Sale Amount* **using** *Aggregation* **Sum.**

Use the INDEX function for ranking data items in views-remember to sort the data in the order of the ranking!

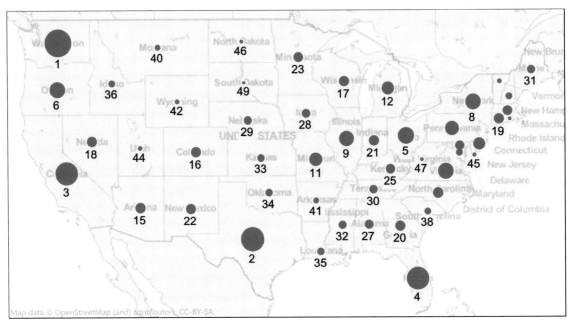

Reference Lines, Bands and Distributions

Reference lines, bands or distributions may be added to your views to emphasize particular values or areas that may be useful in interpreting your data. In particular, when comparing multiple groups or categories of data, reference lines and bands provide immediate feedback on the overall differences between the groups.

Reference lines are vertical or horizontal lines displayed on your view that mark requested values such as average, median, minimum, maximum, sum, total and constants (such as a line that separates the data points as being above or below a target). They can be added on any continuous axis.

Create a new worksheet, <CTRL>+M. Place *Sales* **and the Columns shelf and change the aggregate to Average. Place** *Product* **on the Rows shelf,** *State* **and** *Date* **on the Level of Detail shelf, and format** *Date* **to 'MMMM YYYY'. Change Automatic to Shape and the circle to a plus sign. Right-click on the** *Avg. Sales* **axis. Choose Add Reference Line, change Scope to Per Cell, and click OK. Do this a second time, but change Average to Median and click OK.** If you like, you can change the labels and colors of the reference lines by **right-clicking on the axis and selecting Edit Reference Line, and sorting the view.**

Reference lines for average and median

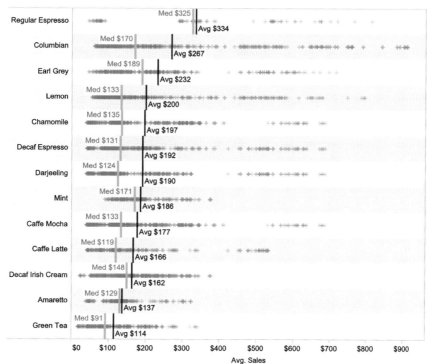

Reference bands are shaded areas, typically highlighting the range of values in a section of the view. They cover the area between two relevant values, such as average and median, or minimum and maximums, which are illustrated in the next example.

Duplicate the prior sheet and right-click on the *Avg. Sales* **axis to select Remove All Reference Lines. Add** *Market* **to the Columns shelf to the left of** *Sales*. **Right-click on the** *Avg. Sales* **axis and select Add Reference Line, choose the Band icon at the top, Scope Per Cell, Band From Minimum to Maximum, and change both Labels to None. You can also format.**

Reference bands for range between minimum and maximum

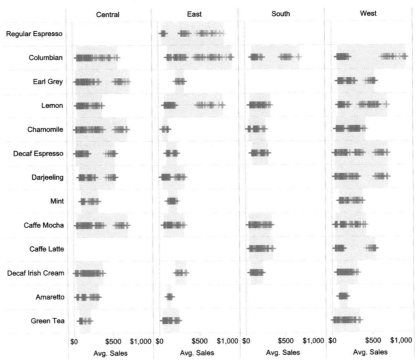

Reference distributions are a modification of reference bands- they typically shade areas above, below and between two requested statistics. The difference is that they represent a distribution of values along an axis, and include confidence intervals, percentages, percentiles, quantiles and standard deviation.

Duplicate the last sheet. Remove the reference line and *Market* **from the Columns shelf. Add Reference Line, choose Distribution, Per Cell, under Computation, choose Percentiles and type in 10,90. You can also change the formatting settings.**

Reference distribution for the 10th and 90th percentiles

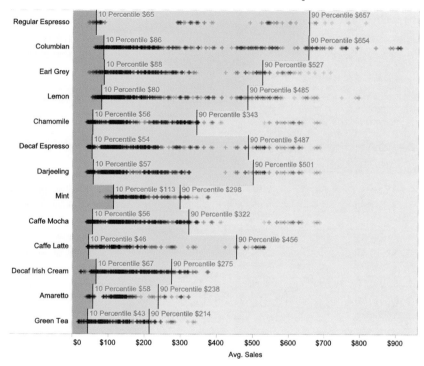

Tableau allows you to customize reference lines, bands and distributions in many different ways, so check out the menus to explore the wide array of options.

Model your data with Trend Lines

Tableau has the capability to model your data with a trend line to help you visualize the overall patterns of the data. The trend line can be based on a linear, logarithmic, or polynomial regression model. Additionally, the trend can be adjusted across dimensional levels so that each pane has a fitted line for the data displayed in that pane. For Tableau to ensure that the math for the trend line is valid, the data items that are on your horizontal and vertical axes need to be equally spaced or have the ability to be converted into a range of continuous values. This includes continuous dimension items, measures added as dimensions, and date dimension items.

Tableau can use trend lines to report significance levels between two variables based on a regression model. Since statistical significance is a complex topic, it will not be described in detail here. One simple way to explain significance is with a p-value, which indicates how well the model fits your data. Lower p-values are better, with values less than 0.05 typically considered "statistically significant", usually written as $p<0.05$.

For example, a p-value of 0.03 tells you that there is a 3% chance that the trend line fitting your data values is describing a relationship between your two variables that is random or does not actually exist (i.e., 3% chance that there is no true pattern and the relationship is just noise). Or stated another way, the probability is that three times out of one-hundred, the relationship described by the trend line doesn't actually exist, while ninety-seven times out of one-hundred, it probably does exist. In Tableau, p-values are available for the entire model, a particular line in a pane, and specific data items used to explain the relationship between your numeric variables.

For example, you may want to try to estimate profit from sales. **Use <Ctrl>- M to open a new worksheet. Add** *Profit* **to the Rows shelf.** Note that the item you want to "predict" should be on the vertical or Y-axis, which corresponds to the Rows shelf. **Next, add** *Sales* **to the Columns shelf.** Turn off the aggregation of data to use all data points in the Trend Line model by **de-selecting Analysis →Aggregate Measures. Reduce the size of the data points to the smallest setting by moving the Size slider on the Marks card all to the way to the left.**

Scatter Graph of *Profit* vs. *Sales*

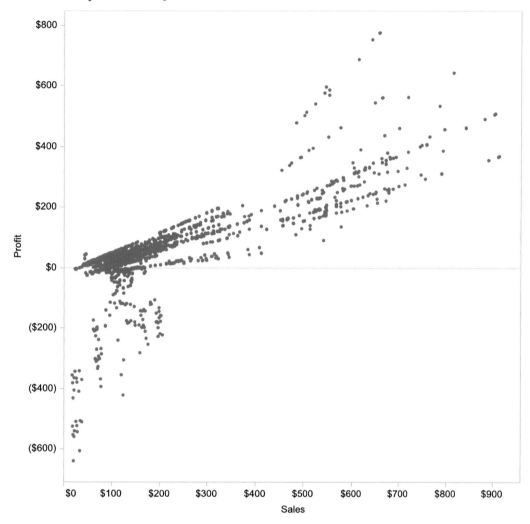

Add a trend line to the view by **right-clicking on the Scatter graph and selecting Trend Lines.** The trend line appears with the default linear (straight) form. To describe the fit of the trend line, **right-click on the Scatter graph again and select Describe Trend Model and** the Describe Trend Model dialog box appears (which you can copy to a clipboard).

Scatter Graph of *Profit* vs. *Sales* with Trend Line

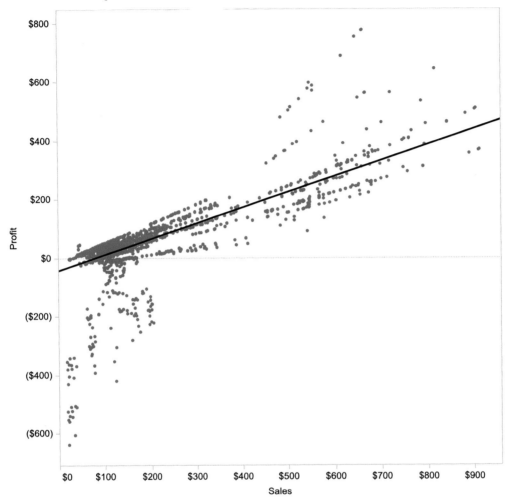

Describe Trend Model dialog box

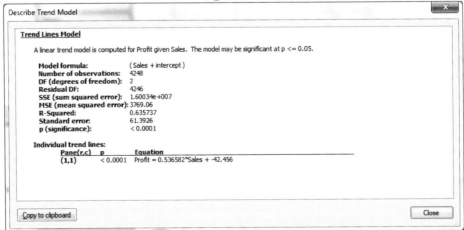

Note that the trend line appears to be drawn across the middle of the data points with some data point outliers towards the bottom left and upper right. There is a noticeable band of data points near the line, so the trend line is a good description of the data, but you can see that it does not perfectly fit the relationship between *Profit* and *Sales*. Note that the Describe Trend Model box shows a significant p-value of < 0.0001. It also shows another very valuable statistic called the R-Squared, which attempts to estimate how much of the data variability is actually explained by the model. In this case, 0.636, or 63.6% of the variability in the data values is accounted for by using *Sales* to predict *Profit*. At the bottom of the pane, you can see the algebraic expression of how *Sales* can be used to estimate *Profit*: multiply *Sales* by 0.537 and subtract 42.5 to estimate *Profit*. This makes sense since you have fixed costs (the intercept, -42.5) and variable costs (you make only an additional 53.7 cents in profit for each additional dollar of sales)! Close the box.

To further refine the trend line, change the type of line fit. For example, try to draw trend lines based on year and market. **Drag** *Date* **to the Columns shelf before** *Sales* **and drag** *Market* **to the rows shelf before** *Profit*. **Finally, add** *Product Type* **to the Color selector on the Marks shelf and keep only the Central region by right-clicking on it in the view and selecting Keep Only.** The Central region is chosen since it appears to have a very strong relationship between *Sales* and *Profit*, shown by the tight grouping of the data points around the trend lines. **Open the Describe Trend Model Box.**

Modifying Trend Lines based on *Year* and *Market*

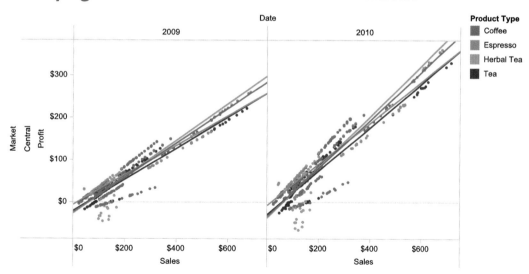

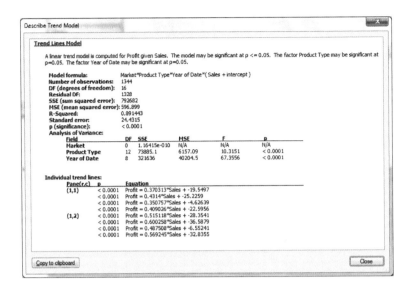

The p-value is still < 0.0001 (highly significant), but the large improvement in R-Squared from 0.638 to 0.891 is exciting. The model accounts for almost all (89.1%) of the variability in actual profit versus expected profit! In real-world business applications, it is rare to see R-Squared values above 60-80%, so this is very impressive. Examining the other fields used in the model, you can see that both *Product Type* and *Year of Date* are significant factors in explaining the model. Each *Product Type* has its own trend line and therefore a unique model describing the relationship between *Profit* and *Sales* for that *Product Type* only.

If you wanted to experiment further with the line type or other aspects of the model, **right-click on the graph and select Edit Trend Lines.** The Trend Lines Options dialog box appears. Here you can change the model type and factors included in the model. You can choose to allow a trend line per color (in this case automatically selected) instead of one trend line overall for all of the colors, or product types in this example. You also can force the y-intercept to zero.

Trend Lines Options dialog box

Concluding the trend line section, we will leave you with some important points to consider about trend line models and statistical analysis:

1) A model with a good fit does not necessarily imply that one variable causes changes to occur in the second variable. For example, a statistically significant model relating temperature with rainfall does not demonstrate that one causes the other to fluctuate, just that the model can describe the relationship between the two. Further knowledge of the process at hand is required to assess if one variable causes changes in the other. The model simply shows they move together.

2) A statistically significant model, indicated by the p-value, can usually be created by adding enough data points. Be sure to examine the R-Squared to see how much of the variability in the data is explained.

3) R-Squared can be skewed by adding more explanatory variables or factors to a trend line model, so try to use a reasonable number of factors to explain the relationship. In general, fewer items that have a high R-Squared are better than many items with a slightly higher R-Squared.

4) Be careful about using this type of model to forecast future values - especially if the external factors around your historic data have changed significantly!

5) If you have several factors in a model that are significant and you would like to remove some to simplify the model, first try removing the ones with the lower SSE values. SSE values measure how much of the data variability is explained by the factor, so factors with higher values for SSE are generally better to keep!

6) Be cautious about turning on the option to set the y-intercept to zero- only do this if you are certain that this condition is true for your problem at hand.

Page intentionally left blank for proper book pagination

Chapter 9

Managing data is critical for great results- Data items and data management in Tableau

---

Chapter Highlights

- Data items

  - Names

  - Types

  - Roles

  - Properties

  - Attributes

  - Custom Relational Hierarchies

- View Data to see what's behind your view

- Bins to group numeric data

- Grouping dimensions into categories

- The power of sets to combine and filter your views

Data management no longer has to be intimidating and confusing- Tableau 6 has made it even easier for most people to manage their data with a wide array of simple yet powerful features. This chapter is very important because effective data management is a frequently overlooked key to analytic success!

Please note that the examples in this chapter use the **Sample – Superstore Sales (Excel)** data source, included with the Tableau application.

Data items: names, types, roles, properties, attributes and hierarchies

Item Names

Item names in Tableau are based on the names in your selected data source. Within Tableau, you can rename items to make them relevant for your audience. For example, the item name "Profit" may seem reasonable for the Marketing team but might not be a specific enough name for the Finance team, who refer to this item as "Gross Profit". Note that renaming an item has no effect on the names in the original data source.

From the Measures pane, right-click on *Profit* **and select Rename from the menu.** The Rename Field dialog appears- **change the name to** *Gross Profit* **and click OK.**

Rename Field dialog box (field refers to your data item)

If you think an item may be irrelevant or confusing, it can be hidden from view by **right-clicking on the item and selecting Hide.** To return hidden items to the view, **click on the down carat next to Dimensions or Measures in the Data Items pane, and select Show Hidden Fields.**

Data Types

Tableau offers five types of data items: ***Number, Date & Time, Date, String and Boolean***. By default, when Tableau connects to your data, it determines which type is the best match for a data item using the data source information and rules around data types. It is important to note that items will behave differently in your views based on the data type.   Typically, you will only need to modify data types when using Access, Excel or text files as data sources. Relational and multi-dimensional databases are usually pre-formatted so that Tableau can select correct data types when you open them.

It is easy to change data types from the item context menu by **right-clicking on the item and selecting Change Data Type.** These are the rules for changing data types:
- Any data type can be converted to *String*.
- A *Number* can be converted to *Date* or *Date & Time*, but this should only be done if your number values meet date convention requirements for your data source.
- *Date* and *Date & Time* can be easily interchanged:
  - Dates simply add 00:00:00 as the time when converted to *Date & Time*.
  - *Date & Time* fields lose their time aspect if converted to *Date*.

To change the default type, **from the Dimensions pane, right-click on Zip Code, select Change Data Type from the menu and select String.**

The Change Data Type submenu

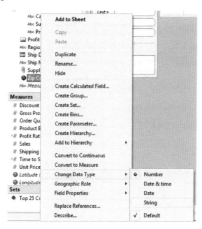

Dimensions and Measures

In Tableau, **dimensions** and **measures** are the primary means of grouping data items in the Data Items pane. By default, Tableau treats any field containing qualitative (e.g., customer type of "New", "Old", "Returning") or categorical (e.g., region of "West", "East") information as a *dimension*. In general, *dimensions* are items used to create row or column headers in a view.

Tableau automatically treats any field containing numeric information as a *measure*. *Measures* typically produce axes when added to the rows or columns shelves. *Measures* are computed using the specified aggregation for each unique combination of row and column *dimensions* used in the view. For example, the data source engine calculates **Sum of Sales** for each dimension item combination (e.g., State and Month) used in the view.

There is an important technical detail to add to this explanation of dimensions and measures. Tableau does not scan the values in your data items, which would be incredibly inefficient. Instead, it uses the metadata provided by your data source to identify and organize your dimensions and measures.

You can convert *measures* to *dimensions* and *dimensions* to *measures*, although more often you will convert *measures* to *dimensions* due to Tableau defaults. You can convert an item from *measure* to *dimension* **by dragging it from the Measures pane to the Dimensions pane, or you can right-click on it and select Convert to Dimension.** You can also perform this action on an item placed on a shelf if you need to convert the item for that particular view only.

For example, you may want to use *Discount* as a *dimension* so you can view all values separately rather than creating an axis from this field. In the following example, **the 1ˢᵗ scatter chart is the default Show Me! view for** *Discount (Measure)*, *Gross Profit* **and** *Region* **(with** *Region* **moved from the shape shelf to the color shelf). The 2ⁿᵈ bar chart is the default Show Me! view for** *Discount (Dimension)*, *Gross Profit* **and** *Region* **(with** *Region* **copied onto the Color shelf).** Notice that the level of detail regarding *Discount* increases after it is converted to a *dimension*. As a measure, it displays one value for each region – the average discount for that region. As a dimension, all the unique values used in each region are shown.

Default Show Me! views:
Discount (Measure) versus Discount (Dimension)

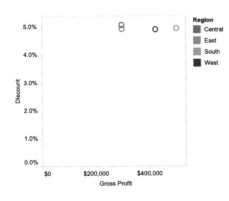
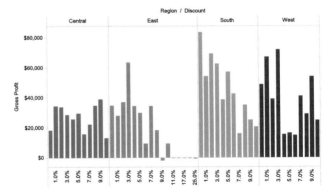

Continuous versus Discrete data items

In Tableau, all data items are classified as either **continuous** or **discrete**. In the Data Items pane, the icons located to the left of all data items are color-coded as green (*continuous*) or blue (*discrete*). When you add them to the Row or Column Shelves, *continuous* items always create axes and *discrete* items always create headers.

You can convert *continuous* items to *discrete* and *discrete* items to *continuous*, although more often you will convert *continuous* to *discrete* due to the Tableau defaults. **Do this by right-clicking on the item in the Data Items pane and selecting Convert to Discrete. If the change is required only for the current view, use the down carat next to the item to select Discrete.**

For example, you may want to change *Discount* to a *discrete* item. In this example, **the 1st continuous line chart is the default Show Me! view for** *Discount (Continuous Dimension)* **and** *Gross Profit* **(with** *Category* **on the Color shelf). The 2nd bar chart is the default Show Me! view for** *Discount (Discrete Dimension)* **and** *Gross Profit* **(with** *Category* **on the Color shelf).** Notice the very different representation of *Discount* as a *continuous* item versus a *discrete* item. The *continuous* graph has no gaps between the discount values, so it displays the long tail from 11% to 25% better than the *discrete* graph, which has separate marks for 11, 16, 17, 21 and 25%. Remember that both *measures* and *dimensions* can be converted from *continuous* to *discrete* items and vice-versa.

Default Show Me! views:
Discount (Continuous) versus Discount (Discrete)

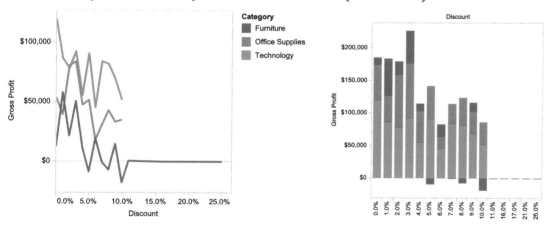

Default Field Properties

All data items have default field properties that can be customized. You can customize them while they are still in the Data Items pane or after you add them to the view. Although there are special field properties for particular types of data items, there are five main ones for most dimensions, **Comment, Aliases, Color, Shape and Sort** and three for most measures, **Comment, Number Format**, and **Aggregation**.

Field properties for dimensions:

- **Comment-** any concise information that you would like to include about the data item, for yourself or others. For example, for Product Category, you may note, "categories were renamed in 2010".
- **Alias-** how the text or labels are displayed, for example changing "NE" to display as "Northeast". Note that dates and continuous dimensions have no aliases since the actual values must be displayed.
- **Color-** affects the default color for values, such as "Exceeds plan" displayed as green and "Below plan" displayed as red
- **Shape** determines the default shape for a value, such as "Exceeds plan" could be ● and "Below plan" could be ◆. Note that only a few shapes have intrinsic color like these special KPI (Key Performance Indicators) shapes. Most shapes use the colors automatically specified for them by the Color shelf.
- **Sort** allows you to establish a default sort order, for instance, manually select the sort order for 'State'. Note that the sorting options are limited versus the Row or Column shelves.

Field properties for measures:

- **Comment-** similar to comments for dimensions, these are notes about the data item that you think are important.
- **Number Format-** allows you to choose number formatting, such as currency as percentage. Some dimensional items, such as Date, can also be formatted.
- **Aggregations-** such as sum or average are available, except for geographic locations.

To modify the field properties from the Data Items pane, **right-click on the item, select Field Properties and pick the property that you wish to edit.** Changing properties of a data item on either the shelves or the view itself will modify the data item's overall properties, unless you have already changed the defaults from the Data Items pane itself. The next several figures are examples of what you can do if you adjust field properties in various ways.

An "audience-friendly" alias for *Order Priority* - default versus customized

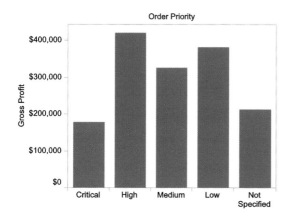
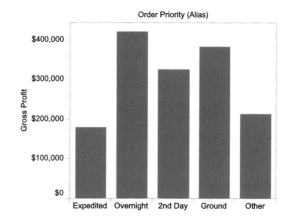

Color for *Order Priority* changed to be urgency-relevant: default versus customized (including manual sort of legend values)

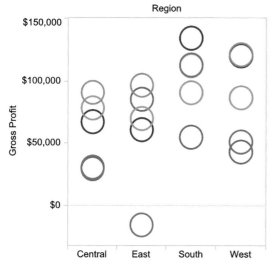
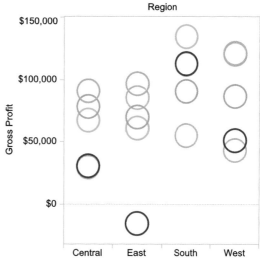

Shape for *Order Priority* changed to be "audience-friendly" based on corporate standards

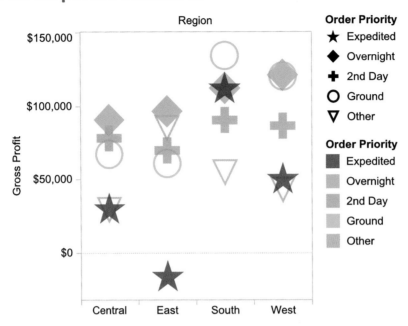

Sort order example: *Ship Mode* sorted by default versus manually

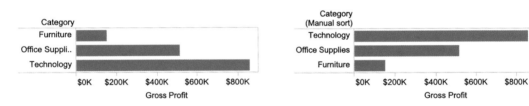

Number format example:
default profit ratio format versus percent format

Aggregation example:
default sum of *Gross Profit* versus *average Gross Profit*

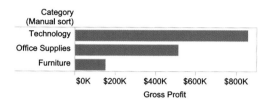 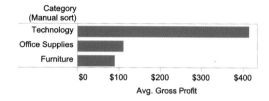

To create this last example, **turn off Aggregate Measures from the Analysis menu to display all records on view. Filter data for top 3 customers by Sum of Sales.** Note that all profit records for these top 3 customers are shown individually versus the aggregated bar chart views above.

Example of no aggregation: beyond default roles

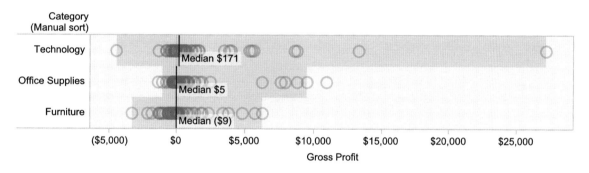

Geographic Roles put your data on the map

Tableau offers exciting mapping capabilities to overlay your data onto relevant maps. By default, data items that have certain names and data types within them are automatically assigned a geographic role. Items that could be one of the following are assigned a corresponding geographic role: Latitude and Longitude, Area Code (e.g., 206, 919), CBSA (U.S. Core Based Statistical Area, e.g., Dallas-Fort Worth-Arlington), Country (FIPS 10 code), Country (ISO 3166-2, 2 character abbreviation), Country (ISO 3166-3, 3 character abbreviation), Country (Name in English), County (U.S. county names), State (U.S. State names), State (Abbreviation, worldwide states and province abbreviations), State (Name, worldwide in English) and Zip Code (U.S. 5 digit zip code). All other items have a default geographic role of None. Additionally, you can add your own geographic roles to extend the capabilities of Tableau, such as the location of your stores or all the airports in the world.

If Tableau does not properly identify your geographic item, you can change this role by **right-clicking on the item, selecting Geographic Role and choosing the proper geographic role from the above list.** Once your data item is assigned a geographic role, it is distinguished with a small globe icon.

In case your dataset has some miscoded items that Tableau cannot map, **you can select Edit Locations from the Geographic Roles submenu to recode these items to their proper values.** See the following example demonstrating this with Zip Code data, which Tableau requires to be 5 digits in length. Miscoded data will appear at 0 degrees longitude and 0 degrees latitude on your map!

Recoding unmatched location data in Tableau

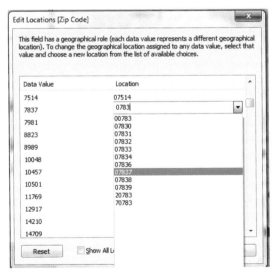

Zip code *Gross Profit* data
before and after mapping-much clearer view!

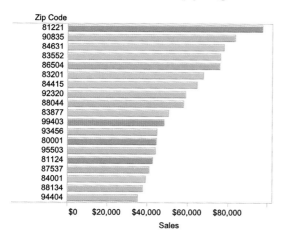

Zip Code

Customer State

- California
- Idaho
- Colorado
- Utah
- New Mexico
- Arizona
- Washington

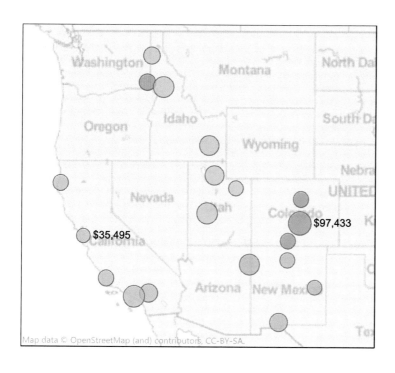

Other Useful Data Management Functions

Other simple data management utilities available from a data item's right-click menu include:

Replace References: this very powerful command will replace all reference to the selected item in your Tableau Workbook with another item. *Be careful, this includes the use of the item in every sheet and in calculated items!* Of course, your views will reflect this change immediately.

Describe: this command will give you very detailed information about the item including role, type, status (is it valid or not?), the formula used for the item and the domain of the item (this is a list of values or a range of values - **you must click Load** to see this, so do not do this for very large lists of distinct values!).

The Describe Field dialog- data item details

Duplicate: this command will perform an equivalent of copy and paste all at once. You will see a duplicate version of the item copied with a new suffix on the item name, typically " (copy)" is appended to the original item name. Note that this does not modify your original data source; it merely creates a new item referencing it. This command is useful for reusing a calculate item formula or having the same item as a dimension and measure simultaneously.

Rename: this command allows you to rename an item with a name more relevant for your workbook.

Hide: irrelevant or potentially confusing items can be hidden from users of your workbook with this command. No changes are made to your original data source when you use this command; the item simply is not displayed in your Data Items pane. Hiding also removes the item from *View Data* and prevents it from being extracted.

Unhide: To unhide items, **click on the dropdown menu beside the icon and select "Show Hidden Fields".** The hidden fields will appear in the pane as grayed-out items. **You must right-click on the item and select unhide for it to be available for use in your workbook.**

Hide All Unused Fields: this command will hide all fields not currently in use in the workbook. This is very useful for simplifying the Data Items pane list from large data sources. To hide all unused items, **click on the dropdown menu at the upper right of the Dimensions or Measures pane and select "Hide All Unused Fields".**

Show Hidden Fields: once you have hidden fields, this option becomes available. Just because you have shown the hidden fields, which appear as light gray data items, does not mean you can use them in views. **You must first right click on the desired fields and select Unhide.**

Sort Data Items: the data items in the Dimensions and Measures panes are sorted by their names by default. If you would prefer to see them ordered by their original data source order, **click on the dropdown menu at the upper right of the Dimensions or Measures pane and select Sort By → Data Source Order**. This is very useful for very wide tables that have the items in a particular order.

The "Sort by" option in the data items pane

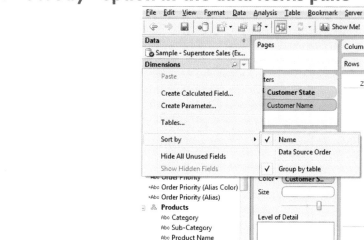

Delete: this command is only available for calculated fields. All other fields can be hidden. The main difference is that once a calculated item is deleted, there is no way to recover it in the current workbook once your session is closed (until then, it can be recovered using Undo functionality).

Comment: you can add comments for data items from **Field Properties → Comment**, as described in the field properties section. Comments appear to users of the data items whenever they hover over the data item field and from the Describe function.

Edit a comment-
hovering over the data item shows the comment

Describe Sheet: this summary is available from the View menu to summarize the details of your current sheet. Information includes a description, mark type, data items on shelves, dimension details, measure ranges and data source details. You can easily copy this information to another application such as Microsoft Word by clicking the Copy to Clipboard button.

Sheet Description box

Custom data hierarchies simplify view navigation

By now, you have seen that Tableau automatically treats date items in your view as a hierarchy, typically starting at _Year_ then _Quarter_, _Month_ etc. You can go down the hierarchy for more detailed views. With Tableau 6, you can also add your own custom hierarchies to rapidly navigate your data. Examples include hierarchies for customer, location and product.

The Superstore Sales sample in Tableau 6 has a pre-built custom hierarchy, _Products_- consisting of _Category_, _Sub-Category_ and _Product Name, which you can see in the Dimensions pane_. To build your own custom hierarchy, **single-click on** _Zip Code_ **and drag it on top of the** _Customer State_ **item in the Dimensions pane**. If you do this correctly, you will see the Create Hierarchy dialog with a default Name of _Customer State_, _Zip Code_. **Change this name to** _Location_ **and click OK.** The new custom hierarchy appears in the Dimension pane.

Adding a custom hierarchy in the Dimensions pane

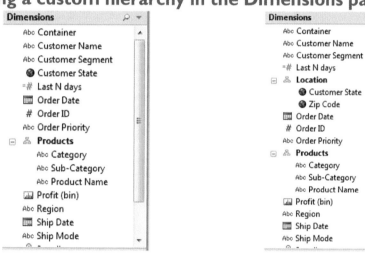

<CTRL>-click on _Customer State_ **and** _Sales_, **click Show Me! and accept the default view type of Map.** You should now see _Customer State_ on the Level of Detail shelf with a + symbol beside the name. **Click it and you will see the map detail go from the state level to the zip code level. Clicking the – sign on** _Customer State_ **will remove** _Zip Code_ **and return to the original level of detail in the view.**

Using the _Location_ custom hierarchy, clicking the + sign on Customer State

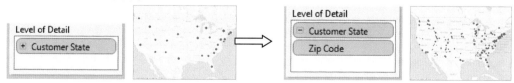

View Data- understand the detail behind the view

This powerful feature allows you to see a table of all records used in your view. **Select specific data points in your view using <Ctrl>-click, or clicking and dragging over parts of the view, then right-click on your view and select View Data.** The dialog box will open. The left tab is the Summary tab, which contains summary data based only on the aggregations displayed in the view. The right tab is the Underlying tab, which contains the rows of data behind the selected data items. This feature is particularly useful for examining unusual data values in your view for additional detail.

Highlighting data points, selecting View Data
Summary and Underlying Data in the View Data dialog box

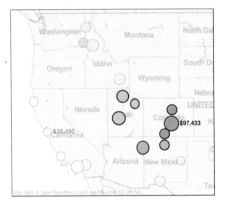
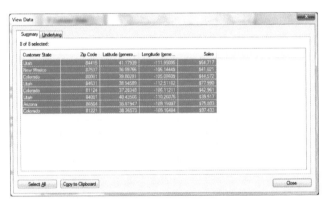

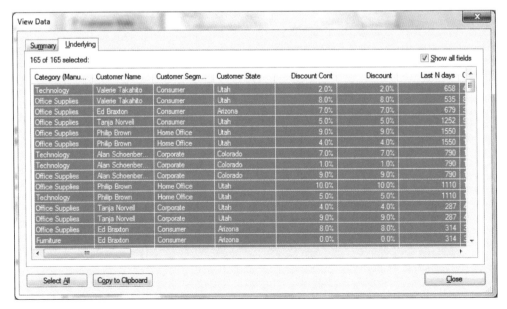

You can resize any field by dragging the side of the header, you can sort by a field by clicking on the header, and you can turn off all other fields not used in the current view by unclicking on *Show all fields*.

As you review the data, **you can select rows with click and the <Shift> key, which allows selection of a range of rows, or the <Ctrl> key, which allows selection of multiple specific rows.** If desired, **you can select all rows by clicking on the Select All button.** Once you have selected the desired rows, you can copy them to your Windows clipboard **by clicking on Copy to Clipboard.** You can paste the results into Excel, Word and many other applications, including Tableau!

Dividing numeric data items into intervals using bins

A data bin enables you to divide a numeric data item into equally sized intervals or "bins". For example, suppose you would like to organize sales transactions into 20 intervals based on sales amount. If you requested to bin sales amount (sales amounts ranging from $0 to $1,000) into 20 bins, Tableau would create bins each having a sales amount length of $50 (e.g., $0-$50, $50-$100, $100-$150, and so on up to $950-$1,000). To do this, you would **right-click on** *Sales* **and select Create Bins**. The Create Bins dialog appears. Unless your data source is very large, you would typically **click on Load** to see the range of values in this field.

The Create Bins dialog for *Sales*
(select Load to see the range of values)

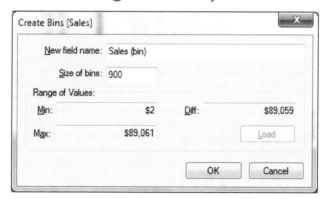

To create 100 similarly sized intervals, **simply divide the difference between the maximum and minimum values (called Diff in this dialog) by 100- in this example, you would use 900 after rounding up, so type 900 in the Size of bins slot.**

! Alternate Route: If you display your data item in a histogram, Tableau automatically bins the item for you.

Bins are very useful for understanding the number of records occurring within each bin (or value range) or examining the total or average value within ranges, as shown in the following examples. In both charts, you can see most transactions are in the first bin and almost every transaction is in the first six bins. The first chart displays *Number of Records*, with virtually every sale in the first bin. Examining the second chart depicting *Sales*, you can see a very different story. While the first bin is still the largest, it is only around 1/3 of the total *Sales*. Therefore, the relatively small number of transactions in the remaining bins yields around 2/3 of all sales dollars.

Sales binned and displayed in two views:
Number of Records versus *Sales*

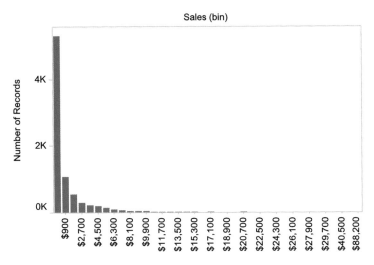

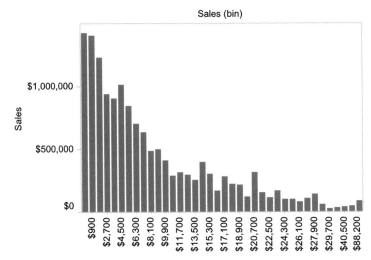

Grouping dimensions into categories

Tableau allows rapid grouping of selected values from a dimensional item. For example, suppose you want to divide product categories into three groups of roughly equal sales to assign responsibility among three new product managers. In the example below, you can see the product categories before and after grouping.

Grouping *Product Categories* into three similar-sized groups to distribute sales volume among Product Managers

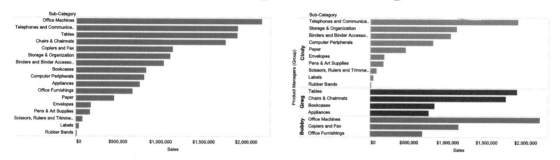

Grouping values directly from the view allows you to leverage the information from other relevant data items. From the view, **select multiple values by <Ctrl>-clicking or <Shift>-clicking *on the headers*, then right-click to select the Group command, or press the paper clip button on the toolbar. Then, you can rename the grouped values by right-clicking on the grouped values and selecting Edit Alias.** The Edit Alias dialog appears, as shown below. **Then click on the values and rename the grouped values in the view.**

Renaming values after grouping from the view

Note that grouping values from the view automatically creates a new dimension item with the same name as the grouped item, with "(group)" added to the name, and changing the alias does not change the name in the dimensions pane. **Add Sub-Category to the right of Sub-Category (group) on the Rows shelf-** this displays the sub-categories included in each group. **Drag Sub-Category (group) from the Rows shelf to the Color shelf,** and your view will be similar to the one shown above (minus a few changes).

Additional grouping functionality is available by **right-clicking on the newly created dimension item from the Data Items pane and selecting Edit** so that the Edit Group dialog appears (shown below).

The Edit Group dialog: Group, Ungroup, Rename, and Group "Other" values

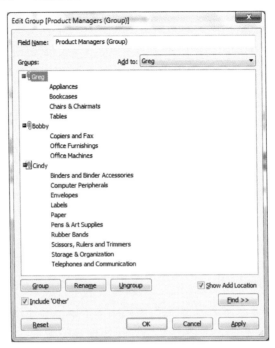

All view-based grouping functionality is available from this dialog, along with some additional features. The view-based grouping approach assumes all values of the data item are available. However, if a new value appears in the data after defining the group, it will be ignored unless you specify where to include the "Other" values, a catchall for values not explicitly categorized. You can ungroup values by **clicking on the group and selecting Ungroup. Then drag ungrouped values to an existing group or create a new group by selecting them and clicking Group.** Another powerful feature from this dialog is the ability to find values within the groups by **clicking on Find**, which expands the Edit Group dialog to add a Find sub-dialog area, shown below with all values containing "office" highlighted.

The Find functionality within the Edit Group dialog

The power of sets to combine and filter your view

Sets are custom fields that are similar to groups but more powerful because they can be created from one or more existing dimension items. All sets can function as advanced, pre-defined filters or placed on the Rows or Columns shelves as data items.   You can have a simple set based on a single dimension item, such as including all order quantities of more than 5 items. A set based on two or more items behaves as a complex item combining all the unique combinations of the selected dimension item levels in your set. For example, a set could contain all sales amounts greater than $80 with a gross profit greater than $40, or all female customers who shopped at our store before 1999.

Three frequent applications of sets include:

- Create a subset of one or more dimension items that can be reused in other worksheets as an item with an automated filter based on the levels selected. For example, **click on** *Sales* **and** *Gross Profit* **and select Show Me!, accepting the default Scatter view type. Add** *Order Priority* **to the Shape shelf and** *Customer Segment* **to the Color shelf**. A chart similar to the figure on the left appears. **Highlight some of the points in the upper right quadrant by <Ctrl>-click,** shown in the right figure. **Right-click on a highlighted data point and select Create Set** and the *Create Set From Selection* dialog appears, also shown. **Name the set "High value customer segments by order priority" and click OK**. The new set will appear in the bottom of the Data Items pane with this special set icon, ⬤ , next to the item.

Create a set from a scatter plot

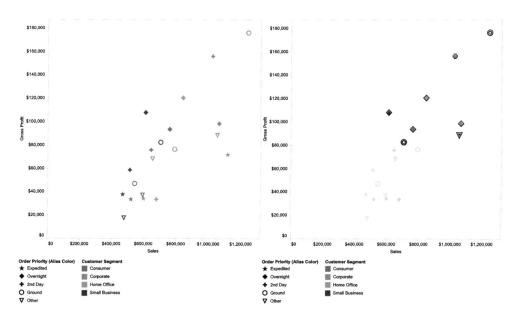

- Create a new set with a unique combination of two or more dimension items. For example, create a set that combines *Customer Segment* and *Order Priority* into a new item. **Click on** *Customer Segment* **while holding down the <Ctrl> key, click on** *Order Priority*, **and then right-click and select Create Set**. The *Create Set from Selection* dialog appears- **name the set "Order Priority and Customer Segment" and click OK**.

- Save an existing filter as a set for later use. Using any of the filter functionality, you can reuse the filter in your workbook repeatedly as a set, a great time saver! Conceptually, this is very similar to highlighting values from a scatter plot and creating a set. To use this capability, **right-click on a filter in your workbook and select Create Set**.

You can use a set just like any other dimension item. You can add a set to a shelf or to filters. However, no matter where you add a set to your view, it is always added as a filter.

! Performance Tip: Note that if you use a filter and a set based on the same dimension, the result will be what the filter and the set have in common (also called the intersection of the two).

Open a new worksheet. From the set creation examples in this section, **add the** *Order Priority and Customer Segment* **set to the rows shelf and** *Gross Profit* **to the columns shelf**- this creates a bar chart similar to the following example. Note that the values are a combination of *Order Priority and Customer Segment* separated by a comma; this is a set functioning as a combination of items. **Now, add the** *High value customer segments by order priority* **set to the Filters**. This updates the bar chart to show only the data for the values selected in the earlier scatter plot.

Sets as a combination of multiple items and a reusable filter

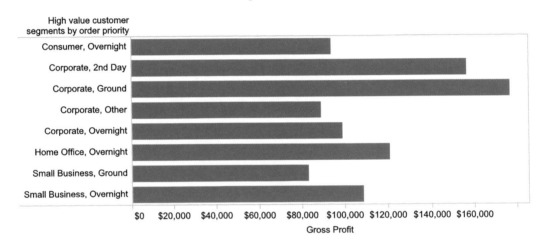

Chapter 10

Advanced data management in Tableau- Calculated Fields, Functions, and Parameters

---

Chapter Highlights

- Calculated Fields- the power to shape your data

- Functions- keys to powerful calculated fields grouped by data type usage

    o Numeric

    o Character

    o Date

    o Logical

    o Type Conversion

    o Aggregate

    o Table Calculations

- Parameters- easily adjust your formulas

In previous chapters, you learned the secrets to great data management using Tableau. This chapter will build upon that knowledge by covering advanced topics such as calculated fields and calculated field operators, the many functions available organized in a table for easy look-up, and the new parameter feature to quickly fine-tune the data that you use in your analyses.

Examples in this chapter use both the **Sample – Superstore Sales (Excel)** and **Sample – Coffee Chain (Access)** data sources that come with Tableau.

Calculated Fields- power to answer your difficult questions

Sometimes you may need a field that your original data source does not include, but that you could calculate using the current fields. For example, you might want to create a new calculated field called Profit Ratio, the ratio of the profit field to the sales field. Another example would be to create a conditional statement called "Shipping Commitment Met" that determines if the actual time to ship was greater than the promised time to ship, returning a value of 1 if true or 0 if false.

To create a new calculated field, **right-click on a field you want to include in the calculation and select Create Calculated Field**. The Calculated Field dialog will appear as shown below. This dialog was also shown earlier in the Custom Table Calculation section.

The Calculated Field dialog

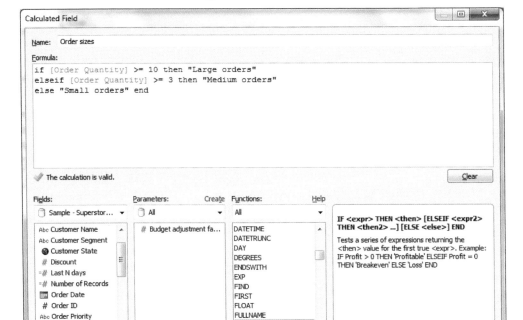

From the Calculated Field dialog, you can name the new calculated field, enter the formula for the new field, add data items from the Fields pane (much better than typing them!), create and add parameters, find functions by category and add them to the formula (the syntax and definition of every available function appears in the lower right hand space when selected.) Using fields and functions, you can create a wide array of simple to very complex calculations to fit a dizzying array of situations.

As you type the formula, text appears just below the formula area indicating if the current formula is "valid". Keep in mind that this is simply checking the syntax of your formula, NOT whether the actual logic you want has been coded correctly! Suppose orders greater than 10 are considered large orders, however, you have typed in >= which is greater than or equal to 10. Obviously, this is an error in your formula, but it is a valid calculation. Carefully examine your formula results in a separate worksheet to verify that it is functioning as expected!

An example of validating the formula above is shown. The new field, Order sizes, is used to examine the Number of Records per size and the Minimum and Maximum Order Quantity for each Order size.

Order sizes	Min. Order Quantity	Max. Order Quantity	Number of Records
Small orders	1	2	316
Medium orders	3	9	1,229
Large orders	10	50	6,854

Examining this table, you would immediately recognize the mistake in your formula logic, and would edit the formula, changing the first line to read:

if [Order Quantity] > 10 then "Large orders"

Yielding the expected values in your table for the order quantity ranges.

Order sizes	Min. Order Quantity	Max. Order Quantity	Number of Records
Small orders	1	2	316
Medium orders	3	10	1,399
Large orders	11	50	6,684

This section contains a detailed list of the Calculated Field Operators and a set of tables that organizes the groupings available in the Functions dropdown from the Calculated Field dialog. Each function includes syntax details and examples using the function.

It is important to note that some functions modify a field (e.g., the left function takes part of the original field and returns it) while other functions test a field or compare fields and return a status back to the calculation (e.g., the length function returns the length of a field while the IF, THEN, ELSE functions check for conditions and returns a value specified by you if true, and another value specified by you if false.)

Calculated Field Operators

To create calculated fields, it is crucial to understand the field operators available in Tableau. The basic operators are shown here in the order of precedence that operator calculations will occur (i.e., addition is calculated by Tableau before any multiplication occurs.)

Operator	Details
+	Addition when used with numbers. Combining or concatenation when used with strings. When used with date fields, it will add the specified number of days to a date: o #June 1, 2009# + 1 will return #June 2, 2009# o " #" marks surround a date value in Tableau (more on this later)
-	Subtraction when used with numbers: o "78-10" will return "68". o [Sales]-[Expenses] will return the gross profit from each transaction from a relational data source. Negation if applied to an expression. When used with dates, subtracts the specified number of days from a date. Calculate the difference in days between two dates.
*	Used for numeric multiplication: 12*7 will return 84.
/	Used for numeric division: 12/6 will return 2.

Comparison operators that can be used in expressions:

Operator	Definition	Example
= = or =	equal to	1=2 is false
>	greater than	1>2 is false
<	less than	1<2 is true
>=	greater than or equal to	1.1>=(1+0.1) is true
<=	less than or equal to	1.1<=1.2 is false
!= or <>	not equal to	1.1!=1.1 is false

All operators can compare two numbers, dates, or strings. They all return a Boolean value, TRUE or FALSE. Note that Boolean values cannot be compared using these operators. For example, FALSE=FALSE is not a valid expression. To compare Booleans with operators, use the logical operators AND or OR. For example, TRUE AND TRUE is valid, returning TRUE.

In the following tables:

- [Number] refers to any number you type (e.g., 7.8 or -14/3).
- [Item] refers to a valid item from your data source.
- [String] refers to a string you type in (e.g., "Tableau" or "Beauty").
- Singular refers to functions that return the same number of rows as your data source.
- Aggregate categories collapse your data to a smaller number of rows based on your view layout.

Numeric Functions (Singular)

Category	Function	Syntax	Example
Numeric (Singular)	**Round a number** to a specified number of digits.	ROUND([Number],decimal) or ROUND([Item],decimal or [Decimal Item]) decimal is optional, [Number] of decimal places	ROUND(10.47)=10 ROUND(10.47,1)=10.5 ROUND([Height],1)= height rounded for each row in the table
Numeric (Singular)	**Check if a number is null, return 0 if it is or the number if it isn't**	ZN([Number])	ZN(2.1)=2.1 ZN(Null)=0 ZN(0)=0 ZN(Null*2.1)=0
Numeric (Singular)	**Absolute value** of a number or absolute value of each value in a database item.	ABS([Number]) or ABS([Item])	ABS(-10.1)=10.1 ABS(18.2)=18.2 ABS([Profit])=all rows in item as non-negative numbers
Numeric (Singular)	**Sign of a number**- negative, positive or zero. Negative is returned as -1, positive as 1, and zero as 0.	SIGN([Number]) or SIGN([Item])	SIGN(-3.5)=-1 SIGN([Sales])= sign for each row in the table
Numeric (Singular)	**Square** of a number.	SQUARE([Number]) or SQUARE([item])	SQUARE(6)=36 SQUARE([item])=square for each row in the table
Numeric (Singular)	**Raise a number to a power**.	POWER([Number],power) or Power([Item],power or [Power Item])	POWER(10,3) = 1000 POWER([LogWeight],2)= weight to the second power for each row in the table
Numeric (Singular)	**Square root of a number**. Returns Null for values of zero or less.	SQRT([Number]) or SQRT([item])	SQRT(36)=6 SQRT([item])=square root for each row in the table
Numeric (Singular)	**Logarithm of a number for a given base**. Returns the exponent needed to raise the base to that number.	LOG([Number],base) or LOG([Item],base or [Base Item]) base is optional, defaults to 10 if not specified	LOG(1000) = 3 LOG([Weight])= logarithm base 10 for each row in the table
Numeric (Singular)	**Natural logarithm of a number**. Returns the exponent needed to raise **e** to that number, or Null if number is zero or less.	LN([Number]) or LN([Item])	LN(7.389) = 2 LN([Weight])=natural logarithm for each row in the table
Numeric (Singular)	**e or Euler's number raised to a power**. **e** is approximately 2.7128 and is commonly used in exponential functions.	EXP([Number]) or EXP([Item])	EXP(2) = 7.389 EXP(-[Growth Rate]*[Time])=**e** to the power of the negative two items multiplied for each row in the table

Character Functions (Modify Items)

Category	Function	Syntax	Example
Character (Modify Values in String)	**Remove all left or right trailing spaces only** (two similar functions).	LTRIM([String]) or RTRIM([String]) or LTRIM([Item]) or RTRIM([Item])	LTRIM(" Cool ")="Cool " or RTRIM(" Cool ")=" Cool" or LTRIM([Item]) or RTRIM([Item])
Character (Modify Values in String)	**Remove all leading and trailing spaces in string.**	TRIM([String]) or TRIM([Item])	TRIM(" Cool data ")="Cool data" or TRIM([Name])
Character (Modify Values in String)	**Upper case** the characters of a string.	UPPER([String]) or UPPER([Item])	UPPER("Stephen 7") = "STEPHEN 7" or UPPER([Name])= names upper cased for each row in the table
Character (Modify Values in String)	**Lower case** the characters of a string.	LOWER([String]) or LOWER([Item])	LOWER("Stephen 7") = "stephen 7" or LOWER([Name])= names lower cased for each row in the table
Character (Modify Values in String)	**Return the 1st n characters** of a string (leftmost characters).	LEFT([String],[Number]) or LEFT([Item],[Number] or [Length Item])	LEFT("Stephen 7",3)="Ste" or LEFT([Name],3)= 1st 3 characters for each row in the table
Character (Modify Values in String)	**Return the middle n characters** of a string starting at a certain character location.	MID([String],start, *length*) or MID([Item], start, *length*) Items can be start and length, length optional	MID("Stephen 7",4)="phen 7" or MID("Stephen 7",4,2)="ph" or MID([Name],3)
Character (Modify Values in String)	**Return the rightmost characters** of a string.	RIGHT([String],[Number]) or RIGHT([Item],[Number] or [Length Item])	RIGHT("Stephen 7 ",3)=" 7 " or RIGHT([Name],3)= Last 3 characters for each row in the table

Character Functions (Locate Values in String)

Category	Function	Syntax	Example
Character (Locate Values in String)	**Test whether a specified string is within a string.** Returns True or False value. This is a case-sensitive function!	CONTAINS([String], specified string) or CONTAINS([Name], specified string) or CONTAINS([Name], [Specified String Item])	CONTAINS("Stephen","J")= False or CONTAINS("Stephen","eph")= True or CONTAINS([Name], "Eil")= False
Character (Locate Values in String)	**Find the position of the 1st instance of a specified string in a string.** Returns 0 if not found. Can specify starting find character location.	FIND([String], substring, *start*), start is optional, or FIND([Item], substring, *start*)	FIND(" Stephen ","eph")=4 or FIND(" Stephen ","eph",5) =0 or FIND([Name],"eph")=location of 'eph' in each row of a table
Character (Locate Values in String)	**Length of a string.** Includes leading and trailing spaces.	LEN([String]) or LEN([Item])	LEN(" Stephen ")=9 or LEN([Name])= length of name in each row of the data
Character (Locate Values in String)	**Test whether a specified string is at the start of a string.** Returns True or False value. This is case sensitive! Ignores leading spaces.	STARTSWITH([String], specified string) or STARTSWITH([Name], specified string)	STARTSWITH("Stephen ","Jo") = False or STARTSWITH ("Stephen ","St") = True
Character (Locate Values in String)	**Test whether a specified string is at the end of a string.** Returns True or False value. This is case sensitive! Ignores trailing spaces.	ENDSWITH([String], specified string) or ENDSWITH([Name], specified string) or ENDSWITH([Name], [Specified String Item])	ENDSWITH("Stephen ","J")= False or ENDSWITH ("Stephen ","en")= True or ENDSWITH([Name], [Specified String Item])

Date Functions

The following examples use the **#** symbol to surround date expressions. This instructs Tableau to interpret the information between the # symbols as a "Date Literal" and convert it to an internal date value (number) that can be used with addition and subtraction operations.   Some of these functions use date_part, which is constant string argument. The valid date_part values that you can use are 'year' (four digit year), 'quarter' (1-4), 'month' (1-12 or "January", "February", etc.), 'dayofyear' Day of the year (Jan 1 is 1, Feb 1 is 32, etc.), 'day' (1-31), 'weekday' (1-7 or "Sunday", "Monday", etc.), 'week' (1-53), 'hour" (0-23), 'minute' (0-59) and 'second' (0-60).

Category	Function	Syntax	Example
Date (Create Item)	**Return the current date or date and time.** Two similar functions.	TODAY() or NOW()	TODAY()=#June 16, 2009# or NOW()=#June 16, 2009 8:10:06 PM#
Date (Item Calculation)	**Calculate the difference between two dates expressed in specified increments.** For example, find the number of months between two dates.	DATEDIFF([Date Unit], [Base Date], [Compare Date])	DATEDIFF('month', #July 30, 2004#, #August 1, 2004#) = 1 or DATEDIFF('month', #July 1, 2004#, #August 30, 2004#) = 1

Category	Function	Syntax	Example
Date (Modify Item)	**Add or subtract a specified amount of date increment(s) to a date.** For example, add 3 months or 3 years to the date.	DATEADD([Date Unit], increment amount, [Date]) [Date Unit] = "day", "week" ,"month", "quarter" or "year"	DATEADD('month',2, #December 15, 2004#) = #January 15, 2005#
Date (Modify Item)	**Return just part of the date as a string.** For example, return the month or the year of a date.	DATENAME([Date Unit], [Date]) [Date Unit] = "day", "week" ,"month", "quarter" or "year"	DATENAME('month', #May 15, 2004#) = "May" or DATENAME('year', #May 15, 2004#) = "2004"
Date (Modify Item)	**Return just part of the date as an integer.** For example, return the month or the year of a date as a number.	DATEPART([Date Unit], [Date]) [Date Unit] = "day", "week" ,"month", "quarter" or "year"	DATENAME('month', #May 15, 2004#) = 5 or DATENAME('year', #May 15, 2004#) = 2004
Date (Modify Item)	**Truncate the date to the start of the unit specified.** For example, truncate a date to the 1st day of a quarter.	DATETRUNC([Date Unit], [Date]) [Date Unit] = "day", "week" ,"month", "quarter" or "year"	DATETRUNC('month', #May 15, 2004#) = #May 1, 2004# or DATETRUNC('year', #May 15, 2004#) = #January 1, 2004#
Date (Modify Item)	**Return the day, month, or year of the date as an integer.** These are three similar functions.	DAY([Date]) MONTH([Date]) YEAR([Date])	DAY(#May 15, 2004#) = 15 MONTH(#May 15, 2004#) = 5 YEAR(#May 15, 2004#) = 2004

Type Conversion Functions

You can covert the result of any calculation to a specific data type. The conversion functions are DATE, DATETIME, INT, STR and FLOAT. For example, if you want to convert a floating-point number like 12.8 as an integer, INT(12.8) would return 13. Note that a Boolean can be converted to an integer, floating number or a string.

Category	Function	Syntax	Example
Data Type Conversion	**Convert a number or string to a date.**	DATE([Number] or string)	DATE("June 18, 2009") = #June 18, 2009# or DATE(#2009-06-18 18:06#) = #2009-06-18#
Data Type Conversion	**Convert a number or string to a date time.**	DATETIME([Number] or string)	DATE(#2009-06-18 18:06#) = #2009-06-18 18:06:00#
Data Type Conversion	**Convert a number or string to an integer.** Before converting to an integer, the value is rounded.	INT([Number] or string)	INT(1)=1 or INT(-1/3)=0 or INT(1.5)=1 or INT(1.50001)=2
Data Type Conversion	**Convert a date or a number to a string.**	STR([Date] or [Number])	STR(#June 18, 2009#) = "June 18, 2009" or STR(1.05)="1.05"
Data Type Conversion	**Convert a string, integer, or date to a floating-point number.** A floating-point number could be 3.000 or 3.1415.	FLOAT([String] or [Number] or [Date]) Note that there must be no commas or other symbols in the value.	FLOAT(#June 18, 2009#) = 39,982.000 or FLOAT("1.05")=1.05

Logical Functions (If, Then, Else)

Category	Function	Syntax	Example
Logical	**PREFERRED METHOD!** Extended logical test to check whether something is true or false repeatedly and return a specified value.	IF logical test THEN true value ELSEIF logical test THEN true value ELSEIF repeat many logical tests THEN repeat true value ELSE unknown value END	IF [Sales] >= [Sales Plan]*1.2 THEN "Awesome" ELSEIF [Sales] < [Sales Plan]*0.8 THEN "Disappointing" ELSEIF [Sales] >= [Sales Plan]*1 THEN "Strong" ELSEIF [Sales] < [Sales Plan]*1 THEN "Just Below" ELSE "Unknown" END For [Sales]=90, [Sales Plan]=100 Value returned="Just Below"
Logical	Simple logical test to check whether something is true or false and return a specified value.	IIF(logical test, true value, false value, [unknown value]) [unknown value] is a catch all if the logical test can't be evaluated, generally due to a NULL in the logical test. Note that it is generally a good idea to use the [unknown value] catchall.	IIF([Profit]>[Budget Profit], "Cool", "Lame", "Huh?") For [Profit]=100, [Budget Profit]=102 Value returned="Lame" or IIF([Items]!=0, [Sales]/[Items], 0, NULL) For [Items]=10, [Sales]=45 Value returned=4.5
Logical	Simple expression checked repeatedly against values to check whether there is a match and return a specified value.	CASE expression WHEN value THEN true value WHEN next value THEN next true value [ELSE catch all value] END [ELSE catch all value] is used if none of the values match the expression used	CASE LOWER(LEFT([Company],3)) WHEN "tab" THEN "Tableau" WHEN "fre" THEN "Freakalytics" ELSE "Another company" END For [Company]="fREakolytcs" Value returned="Freakalytics"

Aggregate Functions

Category	Function	Syntax	Example
Multiple-Date, Numeric, String (Aggregate)	**Minimum** of two values or minimum of all values in a database item, null values are ignored	MIN(date , [Date]) MIN([Number] , [Number]) MIN([String] , string) or MIN([Item])	MIN(1,2)=1 MIN(Stephen, Eileen)=Eileen MIN([Sales]) = smallest sales amount in table
Multiple-Date, Numeric, String (Aggregate)	**Maximum** of two values or maximum of all values in a database item, null values are ignored	MAX(date , [Date]), MAX([Number], [Number]), MAX([String] , string), or MAX([Item])	MAX(1,2)=2 MAX(Stephen, Eileen)=Stephen MAX([Sales]) = largest value in table
Any Data Type (Aggregate)	**Count the number of rows** in a database item, excludes null rows from count.	COUNT([Item]) Unavailable with Excel, Access, and text files. Create a Tableau extract from to use with these data sources.	COUNT([Sales]) = number of sales rows in table that are not null.
Any Data Type (Aggregate)	**Count the number of distinct rows** in a database item, excludes null rows from distinct count.	COUNTD([Item]) Unavailable with Excel, Access, and text files. Create a Tableau extract to use COUNTD with these data sources.	COUNTD([Sales]) = number of unique sales values in table that are not null (if there are 10 sales values but ½ are $5 and the other half are $10, the returned value would be 2.
Numeric (Aggregate)	**SUM** of all values in a database item, null values are ignored.	SUM([Item])	SUM([Sales]) = sum of all values in table, null values are ignored.
Numeric (Aggregate)	**AVG** of all values in a database item, null values are ignored.	AVG([Item])	AVG([Sales]) = average of all values in table, null values are ignored.
Numeric (Aggregate)	**MEDIAN** of all values in a database item, null values are ignored.	MEDIAN([Item]) Unavailable with Excel, Access, and text files. Create a Tableau extract to use MEDIAN with these data sources.	MEDIAN([Sales]) = median of all values in table, null values are ignored.

Table Calculation Functions

Category	Function	Syntax	Example
Table Calculation	Item number from the first item in the table.	INDEX()	On the third column of an across calculation INDEX()=3
Table Calculation	Number of items in the table.	SIZE()	On the third column of twelve SIZE()=12
Table Calculation	Distance from the first item in the table.	FIRST()	On the third column of an across calculation, you are 2 columns past the first location FIRST()=-2
Table Calculation	Distance from the last item in the table.	LAST()	On the third column of twelve, you are 9 columns from the last location LAST()=9
Table Calculation	Running sum, average, min or max of items in a table.	RUNNING_SUM([Item]) RUNNING_AVG([Item]) RUNNING_MIN([Item]) RUNNING_MAX([Item])	On the third column of twelve, RUNNING_SUM(SUM([Sales])) = sum of sales in table from columns 1, 2 and 3.
Table Calculation	Access the table calculation value in the previous item of the table.	PREVIOUS_VALUE([Item]) If it is the first item, then the expression itself is returned.	SUM([Sales]) + PREVIOUS_VALUE(1) = the SUM([Sales]) on 1st item and Running SUM([Sales]) on 3rd item.
Table Calculation	Lookup a value from a relative position in the table.	LOOKUP([Item],Rel pos) Rel pos is an integer to look forward or backwards (negative).	LOOKUP(SUM([SALES]),-3) = the null on 1st item and 1st item value from 4th item.
Table Calculation	Window sum, average, median, min or max of items in a table.	WINDOW_SUM([Item], Start, End) Start is start position in table and End is final position for calculation	WINDOW_SUM(SUM(Sales), FIRST(), LAST())=Sum of all values from 1st to 12th item in a 12 column table. AVG, MEDIAN, MIN, MAX also available

Parameters add additional control for your analysis

A common scenario requested by customers is the ability to quickly adjust budgeting values up or down in Tableau. Parameters enable this type of scenario.

Using the Coffee Chain sample data source, create a new calculated field from *Budget Profit*. **Name this field** *Budget profit (2010 adj)*.

In the Calculated Field dialog, there is a pane in the bottom named Parameters. **Click the Create link right above this field and the Create Parameter dialog appears. Name the parameter Budget adjustment factor, change the Display format to Percentage with 0 decimal points, and change the Allowable values to Range: 0 to 10. Click OK.**

The Create Parameter dialog

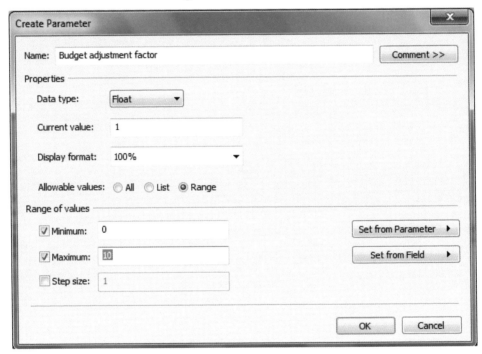

Now you are back at the Calculated Field dialog. **Enter the following formula:**

if YEAR([Date])=2010 then [Budget Profit] * [Budget adjustment factor] else [Budget Profit] end

Click OK.

Create a bullet graph of *Profit* vs. *Budget profit (2010 adj)* by *Product*. **Double-click** *Date* to add it to the view. **Right-click the horizontal axis of the chart and select Swap Reference Line Fields. Click the** *Budget profit (2010 adj)* **data item in the Level of Detail shelf and then click the Descending sort from the toolbar. Finally, create a new calculated field for the Color shelf: name it** *Exceeds goal?* **and use the formula:**

SUM([Profit]) / SUM([Budget profit (2010 adj)])

Add *Exceeds goal?* **to the Color shelf. Adjust the color legend by double-clicking on it, turn on the Use Full Color Range option, click Advanced and Center the legend at 1.**

At the bottom of the Data Items pane, right-click the newly created parameter and select Show Parameter Control.

Bullet graph by *Product* and *Year* with color highlighting enhancement

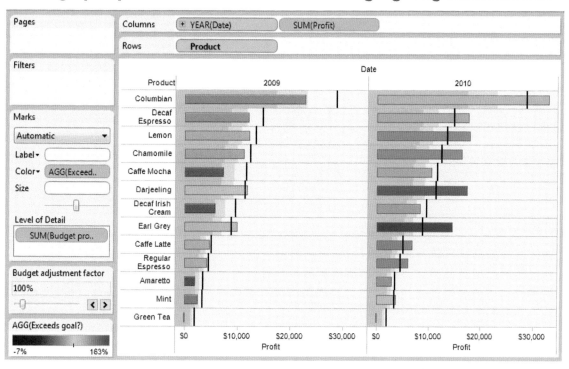

By adjusting the Budget adjustment factor with the slider, you will see 2010 profit targets shift accordingly while 2009 targets remain unchanged (2009 may appear to be changing, but this is due to the adjustment of the *Profit* axis).

Bullet graph with parameter for adjusting targets in the 2010

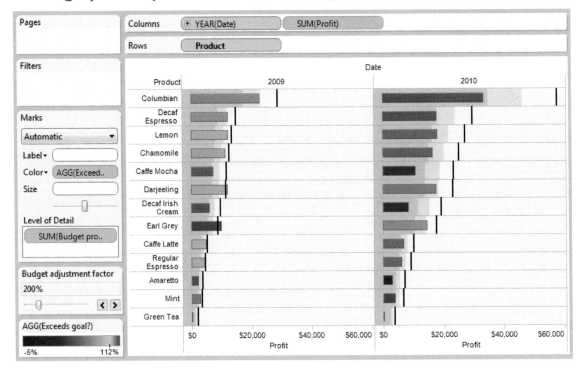

Chapter 11

Advanced data management in Tableau:

Managing data connections

Chapter Highlights

- Queries- from simple to multi-table data queries

- Data blending- use multiple data sources in one view

- Extracts- accelerate your analysis and work away from the office

---

This chapter begins by demonstrating how to query your data, by connecting to a single table in your local data source, or multiple tables if you need data items that have been collected separately (no SQL required!). Then you will learn about data blending, a great new feature in Tableau 6, that allows you to display data from multiple sources in the same view. This is crucial your data are stored in more than one type of system, such as Excel, Access, CSV files and Oracle databases. Finally, Tableau Data Extracts are special copies or subsets of your data that will improve your query performance, allow some advanced capabilities, and analyze your data when you are not connected to your database.

Examples in this chapter use five datasets. You have used the two data sources that come with Tableau in previous chapters: **Sample – Superstore Sales (Excel)** and **Sample – Coffee Chain (Access)**.

The other three datasets can be downloaded and saved from the Freakalytics.com website at http://www.Freakalytics.com/rgts6

1. *The Winery customers and sales* dataset (you may have used this in an earlier chapter)
2. *S and P Ratings* **CSV** data source
3. *Country GDP per Person Euro* **Access** data source
4. There is also an additional tutorial at this location on the web site that covers the basics of building a simple dashboard in Tableau.

Queries to retrieve the data you need

By default, Tableau automatically connects you with single tables in your data source. Some data sources may contain only one table, while other sources have many tables to select from and use as data sources. It is beyond the scope of this book to explain how to connect and optimize the multiple data sources that Tableau can connect with- please see the online help from Tableau for extensive coverage of this topic (**Help → Help Topics**).

Connecting to a new local data source in Tableau is not complicated compared to other applications- if you downloaded and used the winery data from the Freakalytics website for the Motion Chart or Index function examples, you've done it before (snapshots of the dialogs are shown in the chapter with the Motion chart). **If not, download and save *Winery customers and sales* now from Freakalytics.com at** <ins>http://www.Freakalytics.com/rgts6</ins>

On the main menu, **click Data → Connect to Data**, and the Connect to Data dialog appears. **Click Microsoft Excel and Next.** The Excel Workbook Connection dialog appears. **Click the Browse button, navigate to the location of the Excel workbook of *Winery customers and sales*, and select it.** The worksheet names appear in *Step 2: Select the worksheet (table) area to analyze.* **Select Sales data. Keep the default values for Steps 3 and 4 and click OK.**

The Data Connection dialog appears with three choices: *Connect live* (connects directly to your data, *Import all data* (imports entire data source as a Tableau Data Extract) or *Import some data* (imports a subset of your data as a Tableau Data Extract).

Select the first choice- *Connect live*. You are now connected to your data! Then you can save this work as a predefined data connection on the main menu: Data → Data Connection → Export.

This last example accessed data from only one table. However, Tableau allows you to join two or more tables from your data source using custom SQL (query commands written by you!) or via a dialog. Explaining how to write custom SQL is beyond the scope of this book. However, there are many excellent books to learn SQL programming, and some that are specific to SQL specifically for popular databases. Although this book does not cover the details of writing SQL, please note that you can see the SQL Tableau has written for you based on the options you have selected from **Data → Data Connection → Edit → Custom SQL** on the main menu. Learning Custom SQL can be very helpful when working with extremely large data sources (more than tens of millions of records) because you can optimize the query execution with your data source based on your workbook needs. Also, feel free to consult your database team or experts at your company; they may be able to point you to a library of standard queries they have created.

However, the Multiple Tables option from the *Connect to Data* dialog is quite powerful. **On the toolbar, click on the Connect to Data icon. Once again, choose Excel and click Next, and Browse for the Sample-Superstore Sales (Excel) data, which most likely can be found in "My Tableau Repository". Then click on Multiple Tables**. The Connection dialog will change in appearance, shown below on the left. Notice that you already have the Orders table available to you, listed under Step 2. To add a new table to the data source, **click on Add New Table** and the Add Table dialog appears, shown below on the right.

Left- Using the Multiple Tables option for a data connection;

Right- Add Table dialog

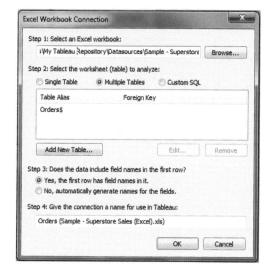 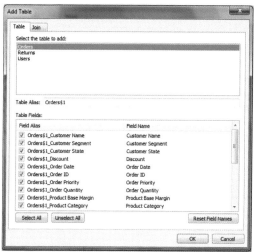

To add the *Returns* table to the data source, **click on** *Returns*. You also must specify a join path; this is how the two tables (*Orders* and *Returns*) will be merged together before returning the data source to you. By default, Tableau will use identically named rows in the two tables to join the data. It also will default to an inner join, which means only rows that exist with the same values will be returned (in other words, rows in *Orders* that don't also exist in *Returns* won't be returned via this data source.) If you wanted all rows returned in the *Orders* table and only matching rows from the *Returns* table, you would select left join instead of inner join. For this example, **select the Join tab, choose Join Type: Left join and click OK** to close the Add Table dialog. **Click OK to close the Excel Workbook Connection, and then choose Connect Live.**

Adding *Returns* to the data source using a left join

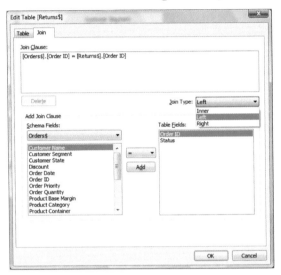

Now, you can build a stacked bar chart. **Put** *Customer Segment* **on the Columns shelf, and** *Sales* **on the Rows shelf twice. For the second** *Sales*, **calculate** *Percent of Sales*, **and make sure to Compute using Table (Down). Add** *Percent of Sales* **to the Label shelf, and Status to the Color shelf.** Since sold orders that were not returned do NOT appear in the Returns table, their status will show up as Null. Change the alias for Null to Sold and colors as shown.

A stacked bar chart of returns (from *Returns* table)
by *Customer Segment* as a *Percent of Sales* and *Sum of Sales*

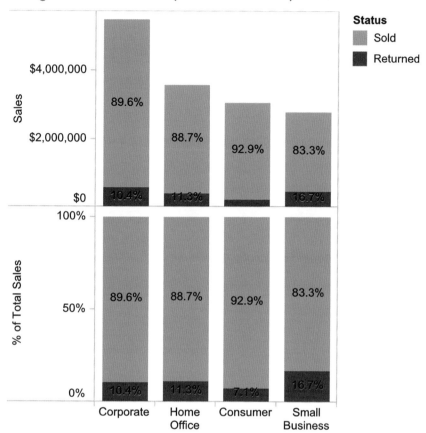

The value "Not Returned" in the stacked bar chart above has been recoded from Null or missing. All rows in *Orders* that did not have a matching Order ID row in *Returns* show the value Null in the data returned from the new multi-table query.

! *Alternate Route*: On the dropdown on Dimensions pane, click on Tables... - the dialog will allow you to add or edit table connections.

One final performance note related to queries. Tableau automatically queries the data source or Tableau extract every time you change the view specification (e.g., changes in marks or shelves). For very large data sources, this is not always preferred since you may want to make several changes to your view before refreshing the data and waiting for your query to complete to update the view. You can toggle the automatic updates feature on and off from **Data →
Automatic Updates or click the** ⌨ **toolbar icon.** If they are turned off, any changes made to the view specification will cause the view to be grayed out until you refresh the data via **Data
→ Run Update or click the** ⟳ **toolbar icon.**

Data blending to use data from multiple sources in one view

A common reality for many users of Tableau is that their data is stored in multiple systems, such as Excel, Access, CSV files, Oracle databases and many other database systems. Tableau 5 allowed you to connect to multiple data sources at one time in the same workbook, but NOT in the same view. In other words, if you had budget data in your Excel data source and actual spending data in Oracle, you had no automated way in Tableau 5 to make a view comparing budget with actuals. Data blending in Tableau 6 was added to the product for scenarios just like this one.

This example uses the **Country Blending** data available on the Freakalytics.com web site. If you have not downloaded the two datasets, **go to** http://www.Freakalytics.com/rgts6 . **Download and save both the *S and P Ratings* CSV and the *Country GDP per Person Euro* Access data sources.**

The first data source is a CSV file containing S&P credit ratings of various countries. The second dataset contains GDP per person in Euros from 1995 through 2009, but only for a subset of the countries in the S&P file. Your objective is to combine country credit ratings with growth rates in GDP per capita for analysis in Tableau.

1. **Connect to the *S and P Ratings* CSV data source. Click the Connect to Data icon on the toolbar, then Create New Connection → Text File. On the Text File Connection dialog, Browse to where you saved the CSV file, click OK, and Connect Live.**

2. **Double-click on the Country data item** (if a warning pops up about missing locations, **check *Do not show again* and click OK**). A map appears with 123 countries displayed.

3. **Change the Mark type from Automatic to Shape, and place S&P Outlook on the Color shelf and on the Shape shelf. The new colors and shapes are shown below. Manually sort the order of the ratings in the legends by dragging them up and down from the legend labels.**

The first data source- International S&P ratings

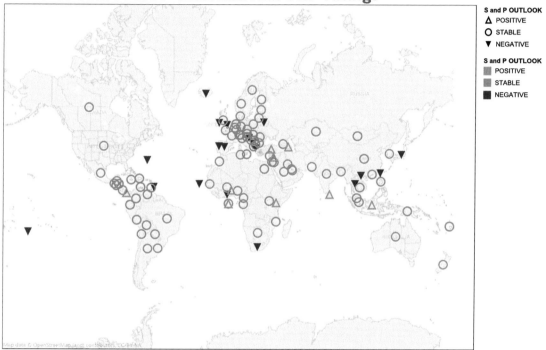

S and P OUTLOOK
△ POSITIVE
○ STABLE
▼ NEGATIVE

S and P OUTLOOK
▪ POSITIVE
▪ STABLE
▪ NEGATIVE

4. **Connect to the *Country GDP per Person Euro* Access data source.** Since you were already using data items from the first data source in the view, this data source is automatically linked to it for blending using the data item(s) in common- *Country* in this case. Notice that a link icon is displayed to the right of *Country* in the new data source. There is also an orange stripe down the left side of the data pane to indicate that adding items from this data source in this view will be achieved via blending.

The link icon and orange stripe to indicate blending

5. **Add** *Y2009* **to the Size and Label shelves.** You will notice that many of the countries have very small data points on the map- this is because they were in the S&P credit rating data source but have no data values in the GDP data source.

6. **To hide all of the data points that are missing GDP per person values, right-click on the** *Y2009* **data item on the Size shelf and select Filter. From the Filter dialog, select Special and then Non-null values, and click OK.** The map will now zoom in to display only countries with GDP per person data values.

Only non-null GDP values displayed

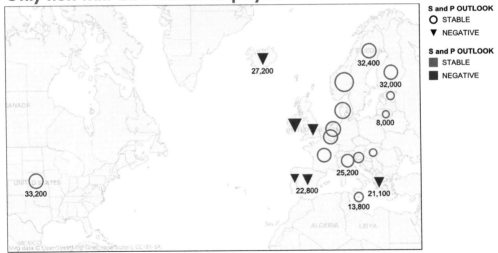

There are two important points to remember about data blending. First, data blending is not part of the data connection definition, it is a behavior specifically activated for a particular view. If you create a new worksheet in the above example, you will see that the blending link icon and orange stripe do not appear until you pick an item from more than one data source.

Second, if you have data items in common between data sources that are spelled differently or misspelled, you can manually specify how they should be blended. To demonstrate this, **create a new workbook and open the two built-in samples included with Tableau- Coffee Chain and Superstore Sales.**

Suppose you would like to contrast sales in each company over time. **Graph the Superstore** *Sales* **data by** *Order Date* **using Show Me!. Then click on the Coffee Chain data source at the top of the data pane.** You will notice that there is not yet a link shown next to any data items in the view (although the orange stripe is visible down the left side of the data items pane). Until you specify a relationship between the two data sources, blending will not occur.

Right-click the Coffee Chain data source at the top of the pane and select Relationships. The Relationships dialog appears.

The Relationships dialog

Click the Custom button, then click Add. Expand *Order Date* **and click on** *YEAR(Order Date).* **On the right side, expand** *Date* **and select** *YEAR(Date) and* **click OK. Repeat these steps for** *Quarter.* **Click OK to close the Relationship dialog.** You should now see a link next to *Date* in the Dimensions pane- this indicates that *Date* is used to link back from the Coffee Chain to Superstore Sales.

Now that you have linked the two data sources, **double-click** *Sales* **from the Coffee Chain data source to add it to the earlier line chart showing sales by year from the Superstore Sales data. Drill down on the** *Year (Order Date)* **item to show quarters. Click the drop-down for the second** *Sales* **item on the Rows shelf and select Dual-Axis.** Now both data series appears in one row with the two items colored. **Next, edit the alias for the color legend names, changing them to "Coffee Chain Sales" (the color with 7 quarters of data) and "Superstore Sales". Format each axis based on the color of the series by adjusting the Shading from the format pane, and adjust the axis scale. Finally, filter on the second** *Sales* **item from the Rows shelf, selecting Special, Non-null values.** Note that only seven quarters of data is available between the two data sources with this last change.

Coffee Chain and Superstore *Sales* after blending

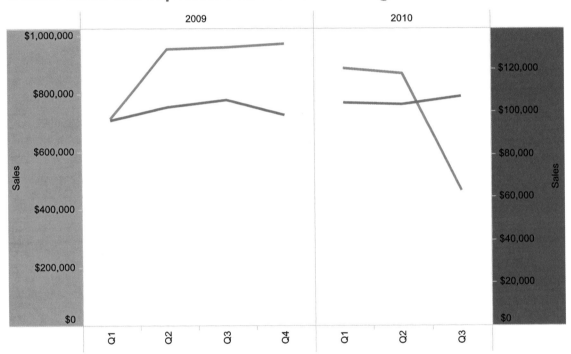

Company results
- Coffee Chain Sales
- Superstore Sales

Extracts to accelerate your data exploration in Tableau

A Tableau Data Extract (the file extension is .TDE on your PC) is a special copy or subset of the whole data source that you can use to improve query performance, enable certain advanced capabilities and perform analysis when disconnected your database. Extracts are typically 5 to 100 times faster than your regular data source and are often 3 to 10 times smaller than local data sources such as Excel and CSV data files. The main disadvantage of extracts is the time required for to build them.

For a simple demonstration of the power of Tableau Data Extracts, we tested some typical queries with a large 950,000 row Excel data table. This Excel data table had 20 data items based on the winery data that you used earlier in the book, and required 60-80 seconds per query on our laptop. The Excel data file size was 105 MB. Generating a complete extract of this Excel file required 90 seconds and resulted in an extract that was 38 MB in size, a storage reduction of 64%. The big improvement was observed in queries using the generated extract, these typically required 0.1-0.5 seconds, 280 times faster! By taking the time to build the extract, you only need to request two queries to make up for all of the time required to build the extract. You also have a much smaller data source and see lightning fast query results for each view request!

You can create an extract with or without filters to include only the data that you want in the extract. Extracts allow you to analyze data stored in large data sources that would slow down your work in Tableau (often multi-table joins can take a while with many databases).

You will be automatically prompted to create an extract after specifying a new data source or at any point from **Data → Extract**. If you create Extracts via the second method, you can limit extract sizes via multiple methods during the extract specification process.

You can also:

- Use field specific filters, for instance, sales greater than $1,000.00 or state="Michigan".
- Aggregate data for visible dimensions, significantly reducing the amount of data stored in the extract based on the current non-hidden data item structure. This is very useful if you have 80 dimensions and have hidden all but a few.
- Roll up data based on years, quarters, months, day, hours, minutes or seconds, significantly reducing rows with transactional data- 50,000 records in a day becomes just a few.
- Take a subset of the data based on the number of records- percent or specified number of rows.

Please note that the last option is NOT the same as a random sample if your data are ordered by date in the data source, it merely grabs data from the "top" of the data source up to the number of rows specified. Also, data sources from certain databases such as SQL Server do add the additional capability to select a random sample, which will show up as another option.

Creating a new data connection
Followed by the Data Connection dialog

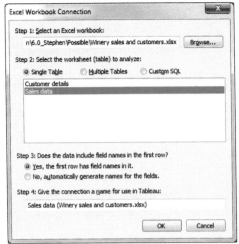
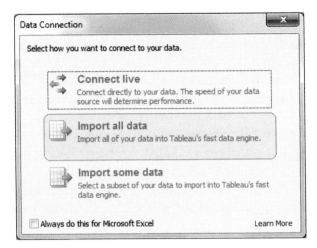

The Extract Data dialog is available when you use Data → Extract Data

After specifying the details of the extract to create, you will need to save the extract to a local file location. Extracts cannot be saved to a network drive for performance reasons. Depending on the size and complexity of your data source and the filters specified by you, extracting data can take a significant amount of time since all of the specified data is retrieved from the data source to your PC. By default, right after you create a new extract, it becomes the data source for the current workbook until you turn it off (**Data → Use Extract**), reconnecting to the original data. Note that toggling the Extract on and off may radically change the data shown in your views if you have added filters in the Extract data dialog.

You can refresh the extract with current data by selecting **Data → Extract → Refresh**. If you want to remove an extract, select **Data → Extract → Remove**. When removing the extract from the project, you will be given the option to also delete it from your hard drive; *do not delete it unless you are certain it isn't in use by other workbooks!*

In summary, these are the key reasons to use extracts:

- When using a file-based data source such as text files, Microsoft Excel or Microsoft Access, extracts radically improve performance.
- Extracts enable additional functionality for file-based data sources, such as the ability to count distinct rows (e.g., how many distinct customer IDs are in the Sales Orders table?) or aggregating a measure with the Median function.
- With large data sources (millions or even billions of rows), you can improve performance and reduce database loads by using extract subsets (e.g., all records for transactions over $1,000.00.)
- To expedite complex Tableau workbook creation (many views) with very large data sources, you can create an extract with a subset of the data to enable rapid view development. Once you have developed the desired views, you can switch to the complete data source by turning off the extract or updating the extract definition.

Page intentionally left blank for proper book pagination

Chapter 12

Sharing your insights from Tableau

Chapter Highlights

- Exporting Images

- Exporting Data

- Print to PDF

- Workbooks and Packaged Workbooks

- Tableau Reader

- Tableau Server

- Tableau Public

Everyone enjoys the company of someone who shares! Now that you have created amazing graphs and gained valuable insights, you are probably eager to share your work with your managers, co-workers, friends and even your family. This chapter will cover many of the capabilities available in Tableau that you can use to distribute your work and make it the talk of the town!

Exporting images is one of the most common needs and Tableau makes it quick and painless. The data used in your view can also be exported to several formats. The ability to print your work as a PDF is very handy for distribution because it can be opened by a widely used document reader found on the internet. Saving work done in Tableau is fast and simple with workbooks. You can also embed the data as a packaged workbook if you need to send it to an external party- they will be able to look at the data behind the pretty pictures. Tableau Reader is a free download that people can use to interact with your packaged workbooks and it includes a subset of the full Tableau product functionality.   Tableau Server is a wonderful product that can easily make Tableau available inside and outside your organization with no installation of software required- all you need is a web browser such as Internet Explorer, Firefox, Safari or Google Chrome. Tableau Public is a free version of Desktop combined with Tableau's free web hosting of your work on Tableau Server.

This chapter uses the **Sample Coffee Chain** dataset that comes with Tableau.

Exporting Images to other applications

Since Tableau allows you to create exceptional graphs, you will likely want to export your gems to other applications such as Word, PowerPoint and other Windows applications. There are three means to export graphs from Tableau:

- Windows copy and paste
- Export as an image file
- Print as an Adobe PDF file (this option is covered in a later section of this chapter)

For the most common uses of exporting images, creating a Microsoft Word report or PowerPoint presentation, Windows copy and paste functionality is fast and seamless. It will work well unless you require images of extremely high quality.

Copy graphs with Windows copy and paste

1. Select **Edit → Copy → Image or <Ctrl> + C.** The Copy Image dialog box appears. The elements available for selection are based on the view type you are using.

The Copy Image Dialog

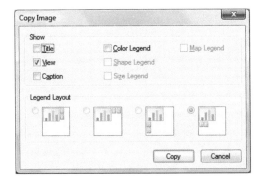

2. Under Show, **select the view elements you want to include in the image**.
3. If you wish to include a legend, **use Legend Layout to determine its location.**
4. **Click Copy**, and the selected elements will be added to the Windows clipboard.
5. To paste a standard quality image of your graph into your Word or PowerPoint document, select **Paste from the Home Menu or the Edit Menu** (depending on which version you have) **or type <Ctrl>-V** (for all versions).
6. For a higher quality graph image, select **Paste Special from the Home or Edit Menu** (depending on your version). **Choose the Picture (Enhanced Metafile) format** to paste the highest quality image into your application.

Export graphs as an image file

1. Select **File → Export → Image**. The Export Image dialog appears, which is identical to the Copy Image dialog except the Copy button is replaced with the Save button. Once again, the elements available for selection are based on the view type you are using.
2. **Select the view elements you want to include in the image.** If you are using a legend, **choose the Legend Location. Click Save.** The Save Image file dialog appears. **Type the desired file name.**
3. Select the file type to use when saving the graph. There are four file types available.
   a. *PNG (Portable Network Graphics):* this is the best choice due to the smallest size and best resolution.
   b. *EMF (Enhanced Metafile):* next best choice, larger size than PNG with best resolution.
   c. *BMP (Windows Bitmap):* third best choice, very large size with best resolution.
   d. *JPEG Image (the default):* lower quality and moderate file size, not recommended.
4. **Click Save.** The graph image file is exported by Tableau based on your selections.

Use copy or export in Tableau to use views in other applications

Exporting Data to other applications and even back to Tableau

Given Tableau's broad functionality, there are few reasons to export your data from Tableau. In case you need this capability, Tableau has several ways to export the data that appear in your view. To export the detailed data *underlying your view* (in contrast to the data appearing in your view), refer back to the "View Data" section in the data item management chapter.

A few tips to consider when exporting data from Tableau:
- The fields exported are the fields that are placed on the worksheet shelves. However, data items on the Filters shelf are excluded unless you also use them on another shelf.
- To include fields without placing them on the Rows, Columns or Marks shelves, **place them on the Level of Detail shelf.**
- You can select all of the data view to export by **Edit → Select All**, or any portion of the data view by **using the <Ctrl> key and clicking on items or by clicking and dragging.** One exception is copying or exporting to a cross-tab, which always uses all the data in the view.

To follow the examples of exports, follow these steps to create this view:
1. **Open the "Sample - Coffee Chain (Access)" data source.**
2. **Click on** *Area Code* **and** *Profit*, **select Show Me! Accept the default view choice by clicking OK.**
3. **Add** *Market* **to the Color shelf.**

Sample view to use with export examples

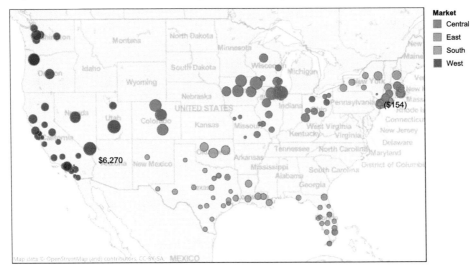

Copy records to clipboard

This method is useful for pasting records into another application such as Excel or Notepad. You must select part or all of the view to use this method. **Drag over the points in Washington and Oregon to highlight them, and then Edit → Copy → Data or <Ctrl> - C**. The records are now available for pasting into another application. Here is what Tableau copies to the clipboard:

Area Code	Market	Latitude (generated)	Longitude (generated)	Sum of Profit
206	West	47.56750603	-122.2772318	$3,823
253	West	47.20133964	-122.4239439	$2,040
360	West	47.03877522	-121.4635792	$1,829
425	West	47.51552986	-121.9352075	$2,017
503	West	45.45323003	-123.2324076	$5,009
509	West	47.34337024	-119.0153828	$1,696
541	West	43.82340572	-120.2964004	$3,378
971	West	45.20118729	-122.7083396	$4,052

Export records to Microsoft Access

This method is useful for large data volumes (greater than 50,000 records) or using the data in Microsoft Access. With Washington and Oregon highlighted, **go to File → Export → Data**. The first Export Data to Access dialog appears. **Type a name for the new Access database file or select an existing Access database file**. **Click Save**. The second Export Data to Access dialog appears, as shown below. Note that you can name the table for use in Access, connect to this export after it is created and select whether the entire view or just the selected parts of the view data are exported. **Click OK** to complete the export. If you keep the defaults, the data exported is identical to that found in the above table.

The second Export Data to Access dialog

Copy or Export cross-tab to clipboard

In the two previous sections, when you copied records from a clipboard and exported records to Access, the data records exported were based on your view selection. These two methods, copying and exporting cross-tabs to clipboards, ignore your selections of marks in the view during export. Also, they both format your export in a simplified version of cross-tabs, but the export method has more attractive formatting.

To follow the next two examples, **add** *Product Type* **to the Level of Detail below the** *Area Code* **item** (this information will appear in the view when you hover over a data point). To copy the view data to a cross-tab format, **click on Edit → Copy → Cross-tab**. The data are now available for pasting into another application, in a format similar to this:

		Product Type	Product Type	Product Type	Product Type
Market	Area Code	Coffee	Espresso	Herbal Tea	Tea
Central	216	$74	$473	$28	$67
Central	217	$672	$682	$68	$319
Central	224	$225	$455	$405	
Central	234	$240	$426	$61	$511

The exported table actually has 156 rows, but the table above shows just the first 4 rows for brevity. This simple cross-tab format is good for use with other applications beyond Excel.

To export this view as a cross-tab to Excel, **click File → Export → Crosstab to Excel**. Note that using this method will automatically open Excel, create a new workbook and place the crosstab export in an Excel worksheet. This method is slower than the copy and paste method. Also, this method does not connect Excel to the data source used in Tableau nor does it place the data in a Pivot Table. An example of the formatting created by this method:

Market	Area Code	Product Type			
		Coffee	Espresso	Herbal Tea	Tea
Central	216	74	473	28	67
	217	672	682	68	319
	224	225	455	405	
	234	240	426	61	511
	262	765	540	960	334
	303	1712	1212	544	459
	309	539	1081	560	389

Again, for brevity, this table has been truncated. Compared to the copy function, the column headers for "Product Type" and the row headers for "Market" are not repeated for each product type or record, respectively, making the table easier to read.

It is important to note that the Export Crosstab to Excel method has much better formatting of the view in Excel than the Copy method. For example, you have to adjust column-widths with the copy method, but the Export method does not require any adjustment and results in a very attractive crosstab.

Print to PDF- export your views to Adobe Acrobat format

The Adobe Acrobat Reader and PDF files are ubiquitous in the PC and Mac worlds. It is only natural that Tableau would use the PDF format as a way to distribute insights created in Tableau.

To print to a PDF file from Tableau:

1. Specify page setup options for each sheet in your workbook, **File → Page Setup**
   a. Key page setup options include
      i. What parts of the view to display
      ii. Show all pages based on the items placed on the Pages shelf (the default is to only show the current page at time of printing)
      iii. Legend layout
      iv. Page margins and centering
      v. Page scaling, e.g., you can fit to 1 pages wide by 2 pages tall
      vi. View title and captions
2. **Select File → Print to PDF** and the Print to PDF dialog appears

Print to PDF dialog

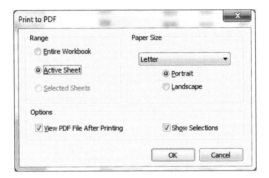

   a. Print Range
      i. Entire Workbook - includes all the sheets in the workbook
      ii. Active Sheet - includes only the sheet currently displayed
   b. Paper size
      i. If you select "Unspecified", the paper size will expand to the necessary size to fit the entire view on a single page
      ii. Other options are based on Windows standard page sizes
   c. Options
      i. Select "View PDF File After Printing" if you want to automatically open the PDF when it is done.
      ii. Clicking on Show Selections will highlight selected data points in the PDF
3. **Click OK**. The Save PDF dialog appears.
4. **Choose the location and file name and click Save.**

Packaged Workbooks- take Tableau on the road!

The vast majority of Tableau workbooks use external data sources. Workbooks can reference file-based data sources such as Excel, Access, text file and even Tableau Extracts. By default, when you save a Tableau workbook, the *connection* information to the data sources is saved in the workbook (but not the data source itself). This means that the next time you open the workbook, the views are updated with any changes made to the external data and any background images you may have used.

In general, saving the workbook with just the connection information is a good route to follow. However, if you need to use the workbook while away from the data source or send it to someone at another organization with no access to your data source, you can include the data source and the background images in a special workbook type - the packaged workbook.

Tableau packaged workbooks contain the workbook, copies of any local data sources, and any background images. Saving the workbook as a packaged workbook also loses any references to the original data sources and images, instead replacing all of these connections with the packaged sources. Note that the only items included in the packaged workbook are local file based sources, such as Excel, Access, text files, Tableau Data Extracts and local database cube files. If you are using a remote database connection, such as Oracle, SQL Server or DB2, you must create a Tableau Extract in order to include these data sources in the packaged workbook.

To save your workbook as a packaged workbook, **click File → Save As** and the Save As dialog appears. **Change the Save as type: dropdown to Tableau Packaged Workbook (*.twbx)**. One big drawback of this approach is that the data size of the actual workbook can grow very large! This is dependent on the size of the data sources being packaged with the workbook. While Tableau uses data compression to minimize the overall size of the packaged workbook, size could still be a problem with data source sizes in the millions of records or larger.

Packaged workbooks are saved with a different Windows file extension than the standard workbook (.twb versus .twbx). If you give this file to someone else with your current release of Tableau, or a later release, they should be able to open and interact with the packaged workbook. One important note: if you share packaged workbooks that contain Microsoft Excel 2007/2010 data or Microsoft Access 2007/2010 data sources, you must have Microsoft Excel 2007, Microsoft Access 2007 or the Office 2007 Data Connectivity Components installed on your PC. If you do not have Office 2007 or Office 2010 on your PC, you can download the data connectivity components from the Tableau web site.

One final technical note! Packaged Workbooks can be unpackaged (much like unzipping a zipped file) at any time from Windows Explorer. You can unpackage a workbook by **right-clicking on the packaged workbook file in Windows Explorer and selecting Unpackage**. Once unpackaging is complete, you will see the regular workbook file (.twb) and a folder containing the data sources and images from the packaged workbook.

Tableau Reader- share packaged workbooks with your colleagues

Tableau Reader goes beyond PDF publishing to allow anyone to view and explore your workbooks. Tableau Reader, much like Adobe Acrobat Reader, is a free product that anyone can install in just a few minutes. The application looks and behaves like the full-featured Tableau product- only the number of features has been limited.

Tableau Reader offers some great capabilities:

1. View and print workbooks or specific sheets, including annotations.
2. Dynamic interaction with workbooks including:
    a. Sorting.
    b. Filtering.
    c. Drilling up and down to change the level of detail in a view.
    d. Rapidly paging through massive amounts of data views.
3. Tableau Reader users can copy and export graphics, crosstabs and data for use in other applications.
4. Interact with view and select outlier data points of interest for detailed viewing or export to other applications.

Tableau Reader- freely available, and includes many of the great Tableau features!

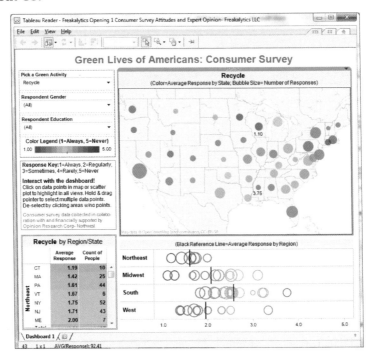

Tableau Server- powerful insights for everyone!

Tableau Server is a powerful extension of the Tableau Desktop product covered in this book. From a web browser, you can use much of the desktop functionality of Tableau across a wide community of users who want to leverage the power of Tableau from the web. Absolutely no installation of software is required and the content can be readily embedded in leading portals such as Microsoft SharePoint. Tableau Server is ideal for the casual user who frequently relies on their subject matter experts for rapid insights and guidance.

Among the many capabilities of Tableau Server:

1. Sharing your interactive workbooks created with Tableau Desktop
   a. Anyone with a browser can easily use your work. Supported browsers include Internet Explorer, Mozilla Firefox, Google Chrome and Apple Safari!
   b. Users can leverage up-to-date data with every view.
   c. Seamlessly embed Tableau views into other web applications.
   d. Publish once with server dynamic data filters data based on user permissions. This is very valuable when you have sensitive data that needs to be limited.
   e. Sort views, and keep or exclude individual data values in your view.
   f. Explore the detailed data beneath the view and export data and images.
   g. Follow links through a guided analysis path to tell a rich story.
2. Collaborate across the team
   a. All users can add explanatory notes, pose questions and suggested answers or simply contribute an opinion.
   b. Review comments to see the discussion around the data.
   c. Publish elegant dashboards to the web.
   d. Leverage powerful tags to organize information in multiple ways.
3. Browse the available views
   a. Quickly identify interesting views by browsing thumbnail images instead of only long-lists of workbook names.
   b. Sort and filter lists of available views to quickly find what you are interested in now.
   c. Powerful content search finds precise and related matches. This includes the ability to search the data structure of the views. For example, you could easily find all views that use "Net Profit" in their execution!
4. Embed
   a. Simple embedding of Tableau views in nearly any web app with standard web link (URL). This method easily provides selected levels of security while widely distributing your analytic information.

Tableau Desktop and Tableau Server

Working from Tableau Desktop, there are multiple ways you can interact with Tableau Server. You can publish to and open workbooks from the server. Workbooks saved to the Tableau Server are centrally available for other Tableau Desktop users in addition to Tableau Server web users.

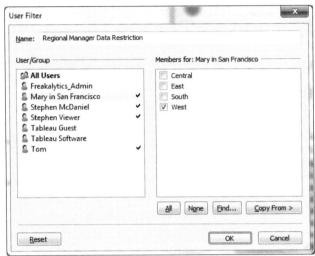

You can import from and publish Tableau data sources to the server. Data sources are available for published workbooks and are synchronized for all users sharing them from Tableau Desktop. This can be a huge timesaver in frequently changing data environments since local data sources do not synchronize back into existing workbooks!

You can specify user or group specific data filters for Tableau Server users. For example, you could allow Tom's dashboard to only include data from the East region and Mary to use just the West region data. To use this capability, you first use the **Server → Create User Filter dialog and specify who can see specific parts of the data.** This creates a Set item in the data pane (based on the name of the User Filter) which must be added to the views in which you wish to restrict data access. This feature should be considered a feature of convenience; all critical security needs should be addressed in your database.

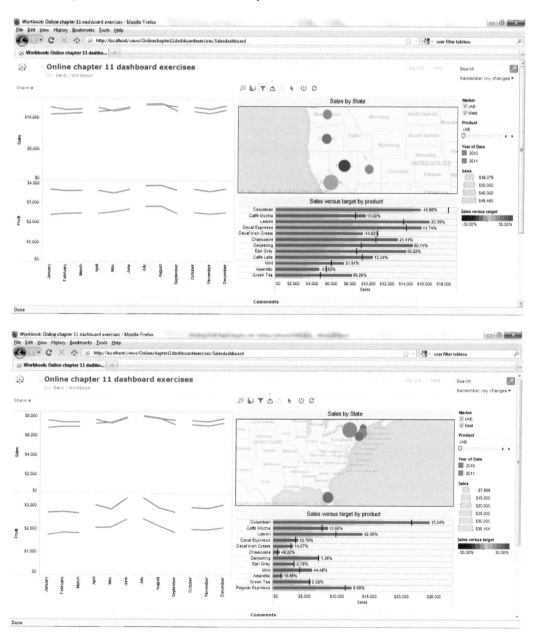

Tableau Public –freely share your visual insights with the world!

Tableau Public is a free version of Tableau Desktop combined with Tableau's free web hosting of your work on Tableau Server. With Tableau Public, you can learn the breadth of Tableau while sharing your insights with the world on any blog or web site. We were excited to be featured on the home page of Tableau Public when it was launched!

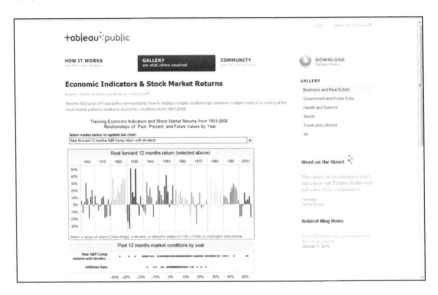

Embedding tableau public content is simple and quick. Your web site visitors do not need to install software to view and interact with your published content, since Tableau depends on native Ajax functionality used by sites like Google Mail.

One of the primary restrictions on the Tableau Public desktop application is the lack of remote database connections- instead you can use Excel, Access, CSV and text-based data sources. Additionally, all work you create in this product can only be saved to the hosted Tableau Public web site (hosted by Tableau Software). This limitation opens all of your work and data as visible to the public. Finally, Tableau Public has size limitations for the total amount of project storage available to your user account (currently 25 MB, about 40 workbooks.)

Publishing to Tableau Public can only occur with projects that are using Tableau Data Extracts, because this minimizes project sizes when published and optimizes performance. You can publish from Tableau Desktop in addition to publishing from Tableau Public desktop- **go to File → Tableau Public → Save to Web As...** You will need a Tableau Public user account and password to publish your first workbook to Tableau Public. Finally, once the workbook is published, you will see options for e-mailing access to the workbook and a separate option for embedding the view on your blog or website. Visit our gallery of examples at http://www.Freakalytics.com/examples or Tableau Public at http://www.TableauPublic.com.

Appendix - Timesaving Tips

Stephen's list of valuable keyboard shortcuts

Keys	Action performed by Tableau
\<Ctrl> + A	Select all data in view
\<Ctrl> + C	Copy selected data
\<Ctrl> + D	Connect to data source
\<Ctrl> + E	Describe Sheet
\<Ctrl> + F	Activate the find command in the Data window
\<Ctrl> + H	Switch in and out of Presentation Mode
\<Ctrl> + M	New worksheet
\<Ctrl> + N	New workbook
\<Ctrl> + O	Open file
\<Ctrl> + P	Print
\<Ctrl> + S	Save file (typically the workbook)
\<Ctrl> + V	Paste clipboard
\<Ctrl> + W	Swap rows and columns
\<Ctrl> + X	Cut selection
\<Ctrl> + Y	Redo undone action
\<Ctrl> + Z	Undo last action (can be used repeatedly)
\<Ctrl> + (←)	Narrow view rows
\<Ctrl> + (→)	Widen view rows
\<Ctrl> + (↓)	Shorten view columns
\<Ctrl> + (↑)	Lengthen view columns
\<Ctrl> + 1	Show Me! Dialog
ENTER	Add last selected data item to the worksheet
F1	Help
\<Ctrl> + F4	Delete the current worksheet or hide it if used in a dashboard
\<Alt> + F4	Closes the current workbook
F4	Page forward playback- starts and stops playback of pages shelf
F5	Refresh the data source
\<Ctrl> + .	Page forward one page- skip forward one page based on pages shelf
\<Ctrl> + ,	Page backward one page- skip back one page based on pages shelf
\<Ctrl> + Tab	Cycle through the worksheets in the open workbook
\<Shift> + F6	Select mode- selects objects in view
\<Shift> + F7	Pan mode- mouse pointer plus dragging moves elements in view
\<Shift> + F9	Zoom mode- mouse pointer plus dragging zooms in view
F9	Run query for current view definition
F10	Toggles Automatic Updates on and off- useful for larger data sources sources
F12	Reverts workbook to last saved version

Standard Toolbar navigation shortcuts

The Select Tool Icon

Click on this icon (highlighted in light blue) to perform the following actions in the view:

\<Click\>	Selects an individual mark w/o retaining prior selection(s)
\<Drag\>	Selects a group of marks w/o keeping prior selection(s)
\<Ctrl\> + \<Click\>	Adds or removes individual marks to the prior
\<Ctrl\> + \<Drag\>	Adds a group of marks to the prior selection(s)
\<Shift\> + \<Click\>	Adds individual marks to the prior selection(s) (only adds)
\<Shift\> + \<Drag\>	Adds a group of marks to the selection(s)
\<Alt\> + \<Click\>	Centers and zooms in, only shows nearby data
\<Alt\> + \<Drag\>	Focuses on the selected area
\<Alt\> + \<Shift\> + \<Drag\>	"Grabs" the view and allows panning/moving

The Zoom Tool Icon

Click on this icon (highlighted in light blue) to perform the following actions in the view:

\<Click\>	Centers and focuses on the point you clicked
\<Drag\>	Focuses on the selected area
\<Shift\> + \<Drag\>	"Grabs" the view and allows panning/moving
\<Alt\> + \<Click\>	Centers and zooms in, only shows nearby data
\<Alt\> + \<Ctrl\> + \<Click\>	Centers and zooms out from the point you clicked

The Pan Tool Icon

Click on this icon (highlighted in light blue) to perform the following actions in the view:

\<Drag\>	"Grabs" the view and allows panning/moving
\<Alt\> + \<Drag\>	Pan/move across multiple panes in a large view

Page intentionally left blank for proper book pagination

Index

A

Aggregations, 109

Aligned Bar, 56

Attainment, *See Bullet Graph*

Axis, 97
Clear and lock, 33
Edit Axis, 97

B

Bar Charts, 56
Aligned, 56
Required Show Me! elements, 52
When to use, 56

Bar With Measure on Color, 60
Required Show Me! elements, 52
When to use, 60

Bins, See Data, Bins

Bullet Graph
Required Show Me! elements, 52
Target vs actual switching, 62
When to use, 62

C

Calculated field, 22, 168
= sign in data pane, 22
Create, 168
Dialog, 168
Formula, 22
Functions, *See Functions*
Name, 22
Operators, 170
Table calculations, 128

Captions, 99

Cards
View (toggle on and off), 33

Chart
Bar, *See Bar Charts*
Bar With Measure on Color,
     See Bar With Measure on Color
Bullet Graph, *See Bullet Graph*
Circle Plot, *See Circle Plot*
Histogram, *See Histogram*
Line, *See Line Chart*
Line (Continuous), *See Line (Continuous)*
Maps, *See Maps*
Pareto, *See Pareto chart*
Pie, *See Pie chart*
Scatter (Matrix), *See Scatter (Matrix)*
Stacked Bar, *See Stacked Bar*

Chart overlay,
See Combination charts

Circle Plot, 64
Required Show Me! elements, 64
When to use, 67

Color-coding, See Marks card

Columns Shelf, 17

Combination chart
Dual-axis (start with), 78
Multiple Mark Types, 78

Combination charts, 77
When to use, 77

Confidence intervals,
See Reference distributions

Crosstabulation, See Table

D

Data

Accelerating, *See Tableau Data Extract*
Automatic Updates, 187
Bins (equally spaced intervals), 43, 159
Blending different data sources, *See Data blending*
Combine, *See Data, Group*
Combine with Workbook, *See Workbook,Packaged*
Combining multiple systems data in one view, *See Data blending*
Connect, 32
Connect live, 184
Connect to Data Source, 116-118, 131, 184
Convert items, *See Functions,Type Conversion*
Country GDP per Person Euro, 183
Custom SQL, *See Queries,Custom SQL*
Export and Level of Detail, 200
Export and Select All, 200
Export to clipboard, 201
Export to cross-tab on clipboard, 202
Export to Microsoft Access, 201
Exported fields, 200
Exporting, 200
Group, 33, 161
Group, all other items, 162
Grouping, *Also see Data, Sets*
Import all data, 184
Import some data, 184
Labels (toggle on and off), 33
Queries, *See Queries*
Refresh (manual), 32
Run Update, 187
S and P Ratings CSV, 183
Samples in book, 183
Save data connection, 184
Sets, 164
Sets, a combination of items, 166
Sets, always a filter, 164
Sets, creating, 164
Sets, optionally shown in view, 164
Sort (ascending and descending), 33
Summary, *View Data*
Swap (rows and columns), 32

Underlying, *View Data*
Update, automatic, 32
Winery customers and sales, 183

Data blending, 188

Based on an item from two or more sources, 190
Example, 188
Link icon, 190
Orange stripe indicating 2nd source, 189
Relationships, 191
Similar to a left join, 192
Specific to a view only, 190

Data items, 144

Calculated, 22
Changing data type), 145
Comment, 156
Context menu, 25
Data types, 145
Default sort order, 155
Delete, 156
Describe, 154
Duplicate, 154
Hide, 144, 155
Hierarchies, custom, 157
Hierarchy, navigating, 157
Multi-select, 18
Names, 144
Options in view (down caret), *See Data items, Context menu*
Pane, 17
Remove from view, 20
Rename, 144, 154
Replace references, 154
Show hidden fields, 155
Swap items in workbook, *See Data items, Replace references*
Unhide, 155
Unhide (Show hidden), 144

Data management, *See Data items*

Data types
Continuous versus Discrete, 147
Convert Measure to Dimension, 146
Convert to dimension, 146
Dimensions, 146
Field properties, Field properties
Measures, 146

Data view, *See Worksheet view*

Dates
Drill down, 19
Hierarchical arrangement, 19

Dual Axis Chart, 64, 71
When to use, 71

E

Exporting results, 49
Adobe Acrobat PDF, 49
BMP, 199
Copy & Paste into other apps, 49
Copy Image Dialog, 198
Dashboards, 49
Image file, 198, 199
Images, 198
JPEG, 199
Paste Special at receiving application, 198
PNG, 199
Tableau Reader, 49

F

Field labels, 99

Field properties
Aggregation, 148
Alias, 148
Color, 148
Comment, 148
Number format, 148
Shape, 148
Sort, 148

File
Save, 32

Filter, 107
Before adding items to view, 35
Condition, 108
Context, 108
General, 107
Hide null values in view, 190
Non-null values, 190
Shelf, 17
Shelves, *See Shelves, Filters*
Top, 108

Format
Dialog, 101
Pane, showing, 41

Formula, *See Calculated field*

Functions
Absolute value, 171
Aggregate, 178
Average, 178
Character, modify values, 172
Check if positive/negative, 171
Convert to Date, 176
Convert to Date/Time, 176
Convert to integer, 176
Convert to number, 176
Convert to string, 176
Count the number of distinct rows, 178
Count the number of rows, 178
Date, 174
Date as day, month or year, 175
Date as name, 175
Date increment, 175
Date modify, 175
DATEADD, 175
Difference between two dates, 174
e or Euler's number, 171
Find string, 173
If then else checking, 177
Leading/trailing spaces, 172
Left, 172
Length of a string, 173

Locate values in a string, 173
Logarithm, 171
Logical test checks, 177
Lower case, 172
Maximum, 178
Median, 178
Middle, 172
Minimum, 178
Natural logarithm, 171
New date item, 174
Now, 174
Null, check if, 171
Numeric, single row at a time, 171
Raise to a power, 171
Return a subset of characters, 172
Right, 172
Round, 171
Specifc part of date, 175
Square a number, 171
Square root, 171
String starts/ends with characters, 173
Sum, 178
Summary functions,
    See Functions,Aggregate
Table Calculation,
    See Table Calculations
Today, 174
Truncate a date to a period beginning,
    175
Type Conversion, 176
Upper case, 172

G

Gantt Chart, 64, 73
    Required Show Me! elements, 64
    When to use, 73

Geographic roles, 152
    Area Code, 152
    CBSA, 152
    Correcting, 152
    Country (FIPS), 152
    Country (ISO), 152
    County, 152
    Identifying items, 152
    In Atlantic Ocean near Africa, 152
    Latitude, 152

Longitude, 152
Metro area, *See CBSA*
Miscoded, 152
Postal code (US only), 152
State (abbreviation), 152
State (worldwide), 152
Zip Code, 152

Graph, *See Chart*

H

Headers, 97, 146
    Edit Alias, 98

Heat Maps, 55
    Required Show Me! elements, 52
    When to use, 55

**Hierarchies, custom, *Data
    items,Hierarchies, custom***

Highlight
    Enable/disable overall, 33
    Enable/disable specifc items, 33

Highlight Table, 54
    Example, 35
    Required Show Me! elements, 52
    When to use, 54

Histogram, 52, 61
    Example, 43
    Required Show Me! elements, 52
    When to use, 61

I

IF THEN ELSE logic, *See Function*

K

Keyboard shortcuts, 212

L

Label shelf, *See Marks card*

Level of Detail, *See Marks card*

Line (Continuous), 64, 66
When to use, 66

Line (Discrete), 65
When to use, 65

Line Chart, 64, 65
Date dimension behavior, 65
Required Show Me! elements, 64

Line Chart (Multiple Measures),
See Dual Axis Chart

M

Maps, 64, 76
Example, 38
Offline (not seeing map), 38
Required Show Me! elements, 64
When to use, 76

Marks card, 17, 87
Changes based on view type, 87
Color, 89
Label, 87
Level of Detail, *See Marks card*
Shape, 92
Size shelf, 91
Text shelf, *See Marks card*

Motion Charts, 116

Mouse
Pan around view (grab and move), 33
Select items, 33
Zoom in and out on view, 33

Multiple chart overlay,
See Combination charts

Multiple Mark Types,
See Combination chart

P

Packaged Workbook, *See*
Workbook, Packaged

Page Filter
Motion Chart, 116
Show History, 122

Pages Shelf, 17

Parameters, 180
Calculated Field access, 180
Show parameter control, 181

Pareto chart, 77

Part to whole with bar chart example,
187

Percentages, 111

Percentiles, *See Reference*
distributions

Pie chart, 64, 74
Issues, 74
Limitations, 74
Negative values, 74
Required Show Me! elements, 64
When to use, 74

Pivot data, *See Data, Swap*

Pivot Table, *See Text Table*

Plot, *See Chart*

Presentation mode,
See Worksheet, Presentation mode

Project Planning, *See Gantt Chart*

p-value, *See Trend Lines*

Q

Quantile, *See* **Reference distributions**

Queries, 184
Accelerating, *See Tableau Data Extract*
Add New Table, 185
Archive, *See Tableau Data Extract*
Custom SQL, 184
Default to single table, 184
Left join, 186
Multiple Tables, 185
Snapshot, *See Tableau Data Extract*
Tables from data pane dropdown, 187

R

Reference bands, 134

Reference distributions, 135

Reference lines, 133

Regression, *Trend lines*

Rows Shelf, 17

R-Squared, *See* **Trend Lines**

S

Scatter (Matrix), 64
When to use, 69

Scatter (Single), 68
When to use, 68

Scatter Plot
Required Show Me! elements, 64

Scatter Plots, 67
Four types in Tableau, 67
When to use, 67

Sets, *See* **Data, Sets**

Shape, *See* **Marks card**

Shelves, 82
Columns, 82
Filters, 85
Filters vs Pages, 84
Page controls, 84
Pages, 83
Pages behavior, 84
Pages vs Flters, 84
Rows, 83

Show Me!, 18, 32
Dragging items on view, 27
Grayed out views, 51

Side-by-Side Bar, 59
Required Show Me! elements, 52
When to use, 59

Size, *See* **Marks card**

Sort, 104
Advanced, 25
Clear, 106
Data item in view, 25
Entire view, 26
Individual rows or columns,
    See Sort, Entire view
Manual, 105
Manual (toolbar), 33
Manual (Toolbar), *See Sort, Toolbar*
Manually from legend labels, 189
One-click Sort, 106
Sort ascending, 104
Sort descending, 104
Sort dialog box, 105
Toolbar (Ascending and Descending), 26

Spotlighting, 112

SQL, *See* **Calculated field**

Stacked Bar, 58
Required Show Me! elements, 52
When to use, 58

Stacked bar chart
Example, 186

Subtotals, 114

Summary Card, 96
Selecting data in the view, 96

T

Table
Highlight Table, *See Highlight Table*
Text, *See Text Table*

Table Calculations
Calculated fields dialog, 127
Compound Growth Rate, 124
Difference, 124
Direction (Compute using), 131
Distance from the first item, 179
Distance from the last item, 179
Item number, 179
Lookup a value, 179
Moving Average, 124
Number of items, 179
Percent Difference, 124
Percent of Total, 124
Previous item value, 179
Quick, 124
Ranking items, INDEX(), 131
Running sum, average, minimum or
    maximum, 179
Running Total, 124
Secondary, 125
Window sum, average, median, min or
    max, 179
Year-over-Year Growth, 124
Year-to-Date Growth, 124
Year-to-Date Total, 124

Tableau
Activate, 13
Beauty, 10
Download, 12
Flexibility, 7
Free, *See Tableau Public, See Tableau
    Reader*
Install, 12

Power, 2
Server, *See Tableau Server*
Simplicity, 9
Speed, 5
Start, 14
Start page, 14
Start Page, 17
Status bar, 22
Toolbar, *See Toolbar*
Trial (14 days), 13
Web access, *See Tableau Server*
Workspace, 16
Workspace controls, 16
Workspace Controls, 17

Tableau Data Extract, 193
Enable additional functionality, 195
Filters to minimize size, 193
Local drives only, 195
Reasons to use, 195
Reduce by date level of interest, 193
Remove, 195
Retrieve ALL specified data!, 195
Sample or subset records, 193
With Tableau Public, 210

Tableau Public, 210
Examples, 210

Tableau Reader, 206
Capabilities, 206

Tableau Server, 207
Basics of working with Desktop, 208

Target and actual, *See Bullet Graph*

Text, *See Marks card*

Text Table, 53
Required Show Me! elements, 52
When to select, 53

Titles, 99

Toolbar, 32
Undo and Redo, 32

Toolbar navigation shortcuts, 213

Totals, 114
Grand Totals, 115
Subtotals, 114

Trend lines, 136
Describe trend model, 137
Edit (modify), 140
Factors, 140
Forecast, 141
Interpreting, 141
p-value, 136
R-Squared, 139

U
User input for formulas, See Parameters

V
View, *Worksheet, See* Worksheet view

View Data, 158
Copy, 159
Navigating, 159
Summary, 158
Underlying data, 158

W
Workbook
Packaged, 205
Packaged contains all local data sources, 205
Packaged requires extract for databases, 205
Packaged- unpackage, 205
Publish to PDF, 204

Worksheet
Clear, 32
Describe sheet, 156
Duplicate, 32
Fit to available space, 33
New, 32
New (add), 24
Presentation Mode, 33

Worksheet view, 17

Made in the USA
Charleston, SC
11 March 2011